7517 1032

P9-CNC-912

BEAVERTON CITY LIBRARY
BEAVERTON, OR 97005
MEMBER OF WASHINGTON COUNTY
COOPERATIVE LIBRARY SERVICES

How Science
CHANGED THE WORLD

How Vaccines
Changed the World

Don Nardo

ReferencePoint
Press®

San Diego, CA

About the Author
In addition to his numerous acclaimed volumes on ancient civilizations, historian Don Nardo has published several studies of scientific discoveries and phenomena, including *Deadliest Dinosaurs*, *Climate Change*, *Polar Explorations*, *Volcanoes*, *Science and Sustainable Energy*, *Robots*, and award-winning books on astronomy and space exploration. Nardo also composes and arranges orchestral music. He lives with his wife, Christine, in Massachusetts.

© 2019 ReferencePoint Press, Inc.
Printed in the United States

For more information, contact:
ReferencePoint Press, Inc.
PO Box 27779
San Diego, CA 92198
www.ReferencePointPress.com

ALL RIGHTS RESERVED.
No part of this work covered by the copyright hereon may be reproduced or used in any form or by any means—graphic, electronic, or mechanical, including photocopying, recording, taping, web distribution, or information storage retrieval systems—without the written permission of the publisher.

LIBRARY OF CONGRESS CATALOGING-IN-PUBLICATION DATA

Name: Nardo, Don, 1947– author.
Title: How Vaccines Changed the World/by Don Nardo.
Description: San Diego, CA: ReferencePoint Press, Inc., 2019. | Series: How Science Changed the World | Audience: Grade 9 to 12. | Includes bibliographical references and index.
Identifiers: LCCN 2018009594 (print) | LCCN 2018010391 (ebook) | ISBN 9781682824146 (eBook) | ISBN 9781682824139 (hardback)
Subjects: LCSH: Vaccines—Social aspects—Juvenile literature. | Vaccination—Social aspects—Juvenile literature.
Classification: LCC RA638 (ebook) | LCC RA638 .N37 2019 (print) | DDC 615.3/72—dc23
LC record available at https://lccn.loc.gov/2018009594

CONTENTS

Important Events in the
History of Vaccines   4

Introduction   6
  The Miracle at Melun

Chapter One   10
  Flickers of Hope in a Disease-Ravaged World

Chapter Two   22
  Discovering How the Immune System Works

Chapter Three   34
  Triumph over a Host of Deadly Maladies

Chapter Four   46
  A Modern Backlash Against Vaccination

Chapter Five   58
  New Research and the Future of Vaccines

Source Notes   70

Glossary   73

For Further Research   74

Index   76

Picture Credits   80

IMPORTANT EVENTS IN THE HISTORY OF VACCINES

1716
England's Lady Mary Wortley Montagu inoculates her son against smallpox.

1881
In the so-called Miracle at Melun, Pasteur demonstrates his successful vaccine for anthrax.

1918–1919
A devastating outbreak of influenza (flu) kills more than 20 million people worldwide.

1798
English doctor Edward Jenner publishes a pamphlet describing his experiments with what he calls vaccines.

1885
Pasteur successfully tests his new rabies vaccine on nine-year-old Joseph Meister.

1921
Future US president Franklin D. Roosevelt is struck by the crippling disease polio.

1750 / 1880 1900 1920 1940

1879
French scientist Louis Pasteur creates a vaccine for chicken cholera.

1908
Russia's Élie Metchnikoff and Germany's Paul Ehrlich share the Nobel Prize for their work in the new science of immunology.

1938
The March of Dimes, a public campaign designed to raise money for research into polio prevention, launches.

4

1955
Millions of American children receive researcher Jonas Salk's successful polio vaccine.

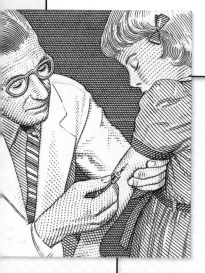

2014
Italy reports an outbreak of some thirty-three hundred cases of measles.

2018
The British medical journal the *Lancet* predicts that genetic engineering technology, which may eventually replace vaccines, is fast approaching.

2007
Appearing on *The Oprah Winfrey Show*, actress Jenny McCarthy claims that her son contracted autism via vaccination.

1950   1970   1990   2010   2030

1986
An effective subunit vaccine for hepatitis B begins to be marketed in the United States and elsewhere.

2016
The World Health Organization reports the occurrence of 216 million cases of malaria worldwide.

2006
The Merck pharmaceutical company introduces an anti-HPV vaccine, Gardasil.

1953
Scientists James Watson and Francis Crick discover the structure of deoxyribonucleic acid, or DNA, which carries the genetic code.

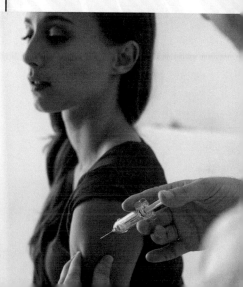

5

The Miracle at Melun

In 1854, when he was thirty-two, French chemist Louis Pasteur took on an assignment that would end up changing not only his career and life but also the world. Hoping to save money and make bigger profits, a group of winemakers hired him to figure out what caused wine to spoil. After a thorough investigation, Pasteur found that wine spoilage was the work of bacteria.

At the time, scientists knew of the existence of bacteria and other kinds of germs, also called microorganisms or microbes. But they thought those microscopic creatures had no significant purpose in nature and assumed that they were harmless. Pasteur concurred with this view until completing his wine spoilage study. If germs could make wine spoil, he now speculated, perhaps they might also harm plants, animals, and people in ways then unknown. Taking a further leap, he wondered whether germs might actually be the principal agents of most diseases.

Pasteur's Chickens

In the three decades that followed, Pasteur continued to harbor this suspicion about germs. One way to confirm it, he realized, was to find a way to cure, or at least alleviate, a disease that germs caused. In this regard, he knew about the work of some earlier scientists in the area of vaccines. A vaccine, says Kristen A. Feemster, a physician who specializes in infectious diseases, "is a substance that is given to a person or animal to protect it from a particular pathogen — a bacterium, virus, or other microorganism that can cause disease. The vaccine prompts an immune response in the body that produces antibodies, which are proteins that fight specific pathogens."[1]

At first, neither Pasteur nor any other scientist understood exactly how vaccines worked. But he knew that these substances had shown significant promise in fighting certain diseases. So he devoted increasing amounts of time and resources to developing a vaccine for anthrax, a lethal sickness of cattle, sheep, and other livestock. Toward that end, he began by examining a similar animal disease — chicken cholera. It was necessary to culture, or grow, the germs that cause the disease in his lab, inject them into test chickens, and study the results.

A major breakthrough came in 1879 when Pasteur learned that as the cultured germs aged, they steadily grew weaker and less harmful. When he injected some of his chickens with the weakened germs, to his surprise the birds did not get sick. Later he injected them with young, full-strength chicken cholera germs. Again, unexpectedly, the chickens remained healthy. Pasteur now realized that the weakened germs were not strong enough to cause the disease but *were* strong enough to make the chickens resistant to it. "Ah, this is wonderful!" he told his assistants. "The secret has been found! The old culture protected the hens against the virulent [lethal] germ. Hens can be vaccinated against chicken cholera!"[2]

> "The secret has been found!"[2]
>
> —French chemist Louis Pasteur after discovering an effective vaccine for chicken cholera

Vital Links in the Chain

Pasteur had demonstrated that vaccination with a weakened form of a pathogen can prevent a creature from acquiring that ailment. Scientists later came to call this the principle of attenuation. Reasoning that the same thing might happen with anthrax,

Pasteur and his assistants began culturing anthrax germs in their lab. They found that heating the cultures weakened the microbes, after which they injected the weakened anthrax germs into some lab animals. Sure enough, the creatures they vaccinated with those germs became immune to anthrax.

Pasteur saw this as a major achievement. But when he told the scientific community about it, most of its members expressed doubts. Moreover, some even scoffed at his work, including the germ theory of disease. A noted French veterinarian, Hippolyte Rossignol, mockingly called Pasteur the "high priest" of that theory. Modern science was not going to believe such things, Rossignol said, simply because Pasteur "has pronounced the sacred words, 'I have spoken.'"[3]

Thinking that Pasteur's conclusions about germs were dead wrong, Rossignol challenged him to prove his theory in public. Pasteur hoped to silence his critics, so he accepted, and the historic demonstration started on May 5, 1881, in a field at Melun, a village south of Paris. A crowd of spectators, among them members of the French press, watched intently. First Pasteur and his assistants vaccinated a group of twenty-five sheep for anthrax. A second group of twenty-five sheep did not receive the vaccine.

On May 31 the crowd reassembled in the field to witness the next part of the demonstration. As the onlookers watched, Pasteur injected all fifty sheep with freshly cultured, lethal anthrax germs. In a few days, Pasteur confidently told the spectators, all the unvaccinated sheep would be dead, while all the vaccinated ones would be alive and healthy.

Early in the morning of June 2, Pasteur was in nearby Paris preparing to take a train to Melun to check on the sheep when he suddenly received an urgent telegram. Sent by none other than Rossignol himself, it stated, "Stupendous success!"[4] Pasteur excitedly hurried to Melun, where, as he exited the train, an enormous crowd greeted him with deafening applause and cries of "Miracle!"[5]

Seconds later Pasteur saw the sheep. Twenty-two of the unvaccinated ones were dead, and the other three were almost so;

French chemist Louis Pasteur vaccinates sheep against anthrax. In 1881 Pasteur demonstrated that his vaccine was a success after his inoculated sheep proved immune to the deadly disease.

yet all twenty-five of the vaccinated ones were alive and well, just as he had predicted would happen. Soon Rossignol made his way through the still noisy crowd and heartily shook Pasteur's hand. The germ theory's most vocal critic now admitted his error and offered an apology, which Pasteur accepted with a smile.

Pasteur did not invent vaccines. Rather, he built on the work of earlier scientists, supplying a vital link in a chain of research that other experts would later add to. These medical milestones included the eradication of smallpox and near elimination of polio and other frightening diseases that once plagued humans and domesticated animals. Today research continues in hopes that vaccines might someday work against cancer and other terrible maladies. Summing up the incredible story of vaccines, Britain's National Health Service calls them "one of the greatest breakthroughs in modern medicine. No other medical intervention has done more to save lives and improve quality of life."[6]

CHAPTER 1

Flickers of Hope in a Disease-Ravaged World

For untold numbers of centuries before the modern age, the specter of death inflicted by dangerous infectious diseases ravaged the human community. Outbreaks of bubonic plague, smallpox, cholera, and many other dreadful maladies regularly killed millions of people and generated large-scale suffering and despair. Moreover, during these long ages preceding the discovery of vaccines, no one knew the root cause of all that misery. Scientists did not begin seriously discussing the germ theory—the idea that germs can cause disease—until the mid-1800s, and they did not unanimously accept it until just before the start of the twentieth century.

Unsanitary Conditions Were the Norm

In fact, scientific researchers did not even know about the existence of germs until the 1600s, when the first crude microscopes appeared. Even then, no one seriously connected these microbes to disease. Instead, a majority of educated people of that era clung to a theory first proposed in ancient times. It held that deadly epidemics were caused by miasmas, poisonous gases somehow formed by mysterious movements of the planets and other heavenly bodies. Meanwhile, a large proportion of the uneducated masses still accepted another ancient belief—that God inflicted disease on humans to punish them for their sins.

Ignorance about the causes of disease was only part of why cholera, smallpox, diphtheria, measles, and other debilitating illnesses repeatedly wreaked havoc on humanity. Another major factor that helped spread these contagions consisted of the unsanitary conditions in which most people lived. In ancient and medieval times, people often dumped human and animal wastes into backyard manure piles, lakes, and streams. Exposed that way to the sun, the solid wastes frequently deteriorated into a powder that winds carried over towns and right into houses' open windows. Researcher Jennifer Wright recounts other problems caused by improper waste disposal, citing common practices in ancient Rome: "Many people dumped their wastes directly onto the streets. The Tiber River [which flows through Rome] was also prone to flooding, which meant [that] a river of [decaying poop] would occasionally flow through the streets. And though people used bathhouses, the water they bathed in wasn't disinfected and frequently contained bacteria."[7]

> "Many people [in ancient Rome] dumped their wastes directly onto the streets."[7]
>
> —Researcher Jennifer Wright

What is more, out of ignorance people tended to spread disease through food preparation and consumption. It was common, for example, to employ unwashed knives to slaughter animals. People then transferred the carcasses and meat to hot, grimy cellars or storehouses that they did not realize were crawling with germs.

Still another widespread unsanitary practice was handling dead, rotting bodies with one's bare hands. Furthermore, during epidemics of various diseases, people frequently threw victims' infected corpses into ponds and streams, polluting those waterways. In all of these ways, disease germs moved freely from

Overcrowded, unsanitary living conditions in ancient and medieval times fueled the spread of bubonic plague and other diseases before the discovery of germ theory.

person to person, household to household, and town to town. It is hardly surprising, therefore, that before the discovery of germs' link to disease and the creation of modern vaccines, diverse and at times lethal ailments struck down millions of people in each new generation.

Early Experiments in Inoculation

The first modern vaccines did not begin to emerge until about two centuries ago. Yet many years before full-fledged and efficient vaccination came about, researchers and even some ordinary people in various countries became aware of the underlying premise behind vaccines. In one way or another, they stumbled on the basic concept that by infecting a healthy person with a sample of a disease, one can provide him or her with immunity to that illness. There was a major problem, however: No one had any idea of how that process worked.

Although not yet conclusively documented, some instances of this immunizing phenomenon may have taken place in China as early as 900 CE. Some historical sources claim that Chinese doctors of that era accidentally discovered the concept of inoculation—the introduction of a sample of a disease into a person's body in hopes of curing him or her. The story goes that they used this method to treat an undetermined number of smallpox victims. *Medical Daily*, an online medical newsletter, sums up this possible early medical advance, saying Chinese physicians noticed that "when healthy people were exposed to smallpox scab tissue, they were less likely to get infected with the disease later on (or if they did, it was a much milder, less dangerous version). The most common form of inoculation in China was to crush smallpox scabs into powder, then breathe it in through the nose."[8]

If the Chinese did use inoculation this early, the doctors who administered the treatment were surely unaware of why it worked. Similarly, a few centuries later various European healers experimented with inoculation without any clear understanding of the principle behind it. Among these observant and daring individuals was the accomplished English poet Lady Mary Wortley Montagu. In 1716 her husband was named British ambassador to Turkey, and she went along with him when he was stationed there.

One reason that Montagu had an interest in combating disease was that she had been badly scarred by smallpox as a child. In addition, that awful malady had killed her brother. This explains her fascination with an event she observed while living in Turkey's capital, Constantinople (now Istanbul). At a gathering of about fifteen people in a local Turkish home, she witnessed a type of smallpox inoculation the Turks called "engrafting." In her lengthy travel journal, Montagu wrote:

> There is a set of old women, who make it their business to perform the operation, every autumn, . . . when the great heat is abated [lessened]. . . . The old woman comes with a nut-shell full of the [pus from] the best sort of small-pox, and asks what vein you please to have opened. She immediately rips open that [vein] you offer to her, with a large needle (which gives you no more pain than a common scratch) and puts into the vein as much [pus] as can lie upon the head of her needle.[9]

Montagu made sure to follow up on the patients she witnessed receiving the inoculations. After a few days, she wrote, they developed fevers that lasted a couple of days, after which they felt fine. Moreover, all of the patients she observed acquired permanent immunity to smallpox. In a journal entry she said, "I am well satisfied of the safety of this experiment, since I intend to try it on my dear little son."[10] Montagu did inoculate her son, who suffered no ill effects. Four years later, after her return to London, a smallpox epidemic struck the city, and out of concern for her daughter's health, Montagu inoculated the girl. Several newspaper reporters and medical authorities witnessed it.

"The old woman comes with a nut-shell full of the [pus from] the best sort of small-pox."[9]

—Lady Mary Wortley Montagu, in a 1716 description of inoculation

Thanks to the publicity surrounding that event, Princess Caroline, wife of the future King George II, took an immediate interest in inoculation in the hopes of protecting her own children from smallpox. To ensure that it was safe, she tested the technique on groups of orphans and condemned convicts. When all of these individuals survived unscathed, the princess had her two daugh-

Jenner Observes Viral Mutations

In a 1798 pamphlet, British physician Edward Jenner described his experiments with inoculation. He also took a moment to speculate about how and why a disease, which he called a virus, might alter its form. He had noticed that horses could contract cowpox, and that the disease seemed to act differently after passing from one animal to another. His conjecture on this point was a very early observation of what scientists now call mutation—the change in form that a disease germ can undergo for various reasons. Jenner wrote:

> May it not then be reasonably conjectured that the source of the small-pox is morbid matter of a peculiar kind, generated by a disease in the horse, and that accidental circumstances may have again and again arisen, still working new changes upon it until it has acquired the contagious and malignant form under which we now commonly see it making its devastations amongst us? And, from a consideration of the change which the infectious matter undergoes from producing a disease on the cow, may we not conceive that many contagious diseases, now prevalent among us, may owe their present appearance not to a simple, but to a compound, origin? For example, is it difficult to imagine that the measles, the scarlet fever, and the ulcerous sore throat with a spotted skin have all sprung from the same source, assuming some variety in their forms according to the nature of their new combinations? The same question will apply respecting the origin of many other contagious diseases which bear a strong analogy to each other.

Edward Jenner, "An Inquiry into the Causes and Effects of the Variole Vaccine, or Cow-Pox, 1798," Lit2Go. https://etc.usf.edu/lit2go.

ters inoculated. They, too, felt no ill effects. As a result of this endorsement of inoculation by a member of Britain's royal family, numerous British citizens sought to benefit from the technique. Subsequently, its use spread across the British Isles and then to both Continental Europe and Britain's overseas colonies, including America.

Edward Jenner and the Milkmaids

The next major link in the chain of discoveries and experiments that led to modern vaccines was the work of a talented British doctor named Edward Jenner. The reason he became interested in the medical principles that would later lead to vaccines is that when he was eight, in 1757, he had been inoculated for smallpox. It had given him full immunity to the disease. The experience had also inspired him to become a doctor and to research ways of eradicating smallpox and other deadly ailments.

One day during some routine research, Jenner happened on what many modern writers call the "mystery of the milkmaids." In his native region of Gloucestershire, in southwestern England, some local farmers told him what he first assumed was an old wives' tale. The farmers claimed that when their daughters milked the family cows, the girls displayed mild symptoms of cowpox, an illness that could be lethal to cows but was mostly harmless to people. That part of the story was not unusual, because in those days it was common for farmworkers to show short-term signs of cowpox.

The difficult-to-swallow aspect of the farmers' tale was the claim that the milkmaids who briefly caught cowpox were thereafter immune to smallpox. Jenner asked some of his medical acquaintances about it, and they assured him that it was nothing more than a superstition. Yet over time Jenner began to suspect they might be wrong. He heard more and more tales about connections among milkmaids, cowpox, and smallpox and reasoned that there might be at least some factual basis for them.

Coining the Term Vaccine

Hoping to confirm his suspicion that cowpox might provide immunity to smallpox, Jenner decided to test it through a scientific investigation. Beginning in 1795, he studied case after case of people gaining smallpox immunity through contact with cowpox and experimented with inoculating various individuals. In 1796, for instance, he inoculated a healthy eight-year-old boy named

16

James Phipps with cowpox pus. Jenner later wrote, "The matter [pus] was taken from a sore on the hand of a dairymaid, who was infected by her master's cows, and it was inserted, on the 14th of May, 1796, into the arm of the boy by means of two superficial incisions, barely penetrating the cutis [outer layer of skin]."[11]

Seven days later, young Phipps displayed minor symptoms of the disease, among them a headache and some chills. "On the day following," however, Jenner observed, the boy "was perfectly well." Next Jenner inoculated Phipps with pus taken from a person suffering from smallpox. Doing this, the man reasoned, would directly test whether the cowpox inoculation had given the boy immunity to smallpox. In his notes, Jenner wrote, "In order to ascertain whether the boy, after feeling so slight an affection of the system from the cow-pox virus, was secure from the contagion of the smallpox, he was inoculated the 1st of July following with [pus] . . . taken from a [smallpox blister]. Several

British doctor Edward Jenner successfully inoculates a young boy with cowpox pus in 1796 in order to give him immunity to the more lethal smallpox disease.

slight punctures and incisions were made on both his arms, and the [pus] was carefully inserted, but no disease followed."[12]

After conducting numerous similar experiments on patients who ultimately acquired an immunity to smallpox, Jenner became convinced that he was on the right track in his battle with the disease. "I shall myself continue to prosecute this inquiry," he wrote. He felt "encouraged," he added, "by the hope of its becoming essentially beneficial to mankind."[13]

"Several slight punctures and incisions were made on both his arms."[12]

—English doctor Edward Jenner on how he vaccinated young James Phipps in 1796

Jenner's experiments were historic. They showed that injecting someone with the fairly harmless cowpox could prevent her or him from contracting the usually lethal smallpox. This method—giving a person a weakened version of a disease to stimulate the body's immune response—was clearly a safer alternative to ordinary inoculation, which carried a higher risk of serious infection and death.

In 1798 Jenner decided it was time to alert the European medical community to his achievement. To that end, he published a sixty-four-page pamphlet describing his experiments. In the text, he referred to his discovery as a vaccine, after the Latin name for cowpox—*Variolae vaccinae*. During the decades that followed, in his honor, *vaccine* became the universal term for an immunizing substance used in the manner he had demonstrated.

A Certainty That Germs Cause Disease

The immediate reactions within the scientific community to Jenner's findings were mixed. Some medical researchers felt that his vaccine treatment sounded promising. Perhaps, they suggested, it might be a flicker of hope in a disease-ravaged world. Conversely, quite a few others were highly critical, and some went so far as to suggest he was wasting his time trying to prove the reality of a mere superstition.

This initial negative conclusion proved premature, however. During the ensuing decades doctors and other researchers in

Britain, France, and other European countries repeated Jenner's experiments with the same positive outcomes. As a result, Jenner's method of vaccinating people swiftly became the preferred method for treating smallpox.

At the time, the major lingering problem with the technique and the research behind it was that no one yet understood exactly why vaccination worked. The principal reason for this was that science had not yet firmly linked bacteria, viruses, and other germs with disease.

It was Frenchman Louis Pasteur's work that began to establish that crucial connection. His 1854 experiments demonstrating that bacteria caused wine to spoil inspired his strong suspicion that microbes might also cause various diseases.

Pasteur and the Spoiled Wine

When in 1854 a group of winemakers asked Louis Pasteur to discover what caused wine to spoil, he employed a simple but ingenious approach. First he examined a drop of normal wine through his microscope, and then he did the same with some spoiled wine. Both samples, he noted, contained numerous oval-shaped germs called yeasts. In the spoiled wine alone, however, Pasteur observed large numbers of smaller microbes that scientists called bacteria. At the time, experts assumed that bacteria, and yeasts too, were harmless and suddenly came into existence as a result of the process of fermentation, which makes grape juice turn into wine. One day it occurred to Pasteur that perhaps the bacteria did *not* appear from nowhere during fermentation. Moreover, maybe they were not harmless after all. In addition, he mused, what if the yeasts were not created by fermentation but rather *caused* it? To test these ideas, he heated some fresh grape juice containing yeasts until the yeasts were dead and saw that the juice did not turn into wine. But when he added some yeasts to the juice, it *did* ferment normally. This showed clearly that yeasts actually cause fermentation. Pasteur also took some freshly fermented wine and made sure it remained tightly sealed. Because bacteria could not get in, he realized, the sealed wine remained unspoiled. Next he purposely added some of the bacteria to the fresh wine, which swiftly spoiled. Quickly and brilliantly, Pasteur proved that some germs initiate fermentation whereas others cause spoilage.

Pasteur was well aware of Jenner's work and the subsequent widespread use of a vaccine to prevent smallpox. In theory, Pasteur reasoned, smallpox was caused by a specific kind of germ, and the same was true of many other deadly diseases. Moreover, he posited, since a vaccine had been shown to prevent smallpox, other diseases should also be treatable with vaccines. This is a simplified summary of the thought process that led Pasteur to develop his vaccine for anthrax. His historic demonstration of its effectiveness in 1881 in the French village of Melun confirmed for him that germs were the culprits behind various diseases and that vaccines were a viable way to fight those maladies.

In addition, Pasteur's work with anthrax had proved that a vaccine containing a weakened, or attenuated, form of a disease germ provided protection against that disease. At least it did so for animals. He assumed that logically the same approach should work on people, but without clear-cut evidence, he could not be absolutely certain. Thus, he decided, the next step must be to develop and test a vaccine for a disease that commonly plagued humans.

Pasteur, Rabies, and Generations Yet Unborn

For this line of research, Pasteur chose hydrophobia, more often called rabies, a potentially fatal illness that people usually contract from animal bites. Using his microscope, he initially searched for but could not find the rabies microbes he was sure existed. Finally, he correctly concluded that the rabies germs were invisible because they were far tinier than the bacteria he was accustomed to dealing with. (Years later, other scientists confirmed the existence of those smaller germs and named them viruses.)

Even though Pasteur could not see the rabies viruses, he wisely carried on his work under the hypothesis that they were real. After more than four years, he managed to attenuate the rabies germs. He then tested his vaccine on 125 dogs, all of which gained immunity to the disease.

In March 1885 Pasteur was ready to test the vaccine on a human subject. At first he considered vaccinating himself. But soon

Louis Pasteur studies the rabies germ in his laboratory. In 1885 he showed that his attenuated rabies vaccine could be used to cure people who were infected with the disease.

the mother of a nine-year-old boy named Joseph Meister, who had been bitten by a rabid dog, begged the scientist for help. Leaping into action, Pasteur prepared the vaccine. He knew that because he was not a medical doctor, it was illegal for him to treat humans, so he asked an associate, Dr. Jacques Grancher, to administer the injection. The boy received twelve shots over a period of ten days. Thereafter, even after the passage of several months, Meister displayed complete immunity to rabies. In one of the great triumphs of modern science, Pasteur had shown that attenuated vaccines could be used successfully to treat infected humans.

Pasteur's work on microbes and attenuated vaccines opened the way for scientists to develop new vaccines to fight a number of other diseases. As humble as he was brilliant, he declared that he owed much of his success to Jenner. Other researchers agreed that Jenner's work had been key. But so was Pasteur's, they insisted, and thereafter science placed him on the pedestal he had rightfully earned. Together, Jenner and Pasteur made possible the development of numerous vaccines in the twentieth century and beyond; thereby, their ingenuity and dedication indirectly saved hundreds of millions of lives in generations yet unborn.

CHAPTER 2

Discovering How the Immune System Works

Building on the work of Edward Jenner, Louis Pasteur, and other pioneers, in the late 1800s and early 1900s, a new medical science emerged—immunology, the study of how the immune system works. Because they work by stimulating the body to fight off various diseases, vaccines became and remain a major branch of immunology. Throughout the twentieth century, universities, national governments, and private charities alike provided funding for research into new kinds of vaccines. Thousands of medical researchers—young and old, male and female, and in countries around the world—devoted their lives to unlocking the secrets of immunity. This enormous and at times heroic effort led to the eradication or near conquest of many once-lethal or crippling diseases. Among them was polio, which in the past had robbed hundreds of thousands of children and grownups of the ability to walk and lead normal lives.

The Body's Disease-Fighting Cells

None of these modern vaccine-related achievements would have been possible without an understanding of how the body's immune system works. In fact, solving that mystery became one of the biggest challenges for medical researchers in the years following Pasteur's work on anthrax and rabies. One key player in this groundbreaking research was Russian biologist Élie Metchnikoff. He studied the workings of immunity by himself in Russia before joining the Pasteur Institute in Paris in 1888. Another early major contributor to knowledge of immunity was Germany's Paul Ehrlich. In only a little more than two decades, those two scientists, aided by a few others, uncovered many of the basics of immunology, and for their work in that area Metchnikoff and Ehrlich shared the Nobel Prize in Physiology or Medicine in 1908. Other researchers later clarified and/or added detail to their explanation of how both the body and vaccines fight off disease pathogens.

According to that basic explanation of the immune system, a vaccine motivates the body to mount a defense against harmful substances, or antigens, that invade from the outside. Scientists call such a defense an immune response. It consists of the speedy creation of disease-fighting cells and other microscopic particles, which attack and destroy alien antigens. Among those defensive cells are lymphocytes, white blood cells that grow in the bone marrow. One type of lymphocyte, the B cell, manufactures and releases proteins called antibodies; another white blood cell, the T cell, helps the B cell produce antibodies.

Once released, millions of antibodies converge on the area where the disease antigens entered the body. Some of the antibodies cause chemical changes in the antigens, making them fall apart. Other antibodies surround and latch on to the antigens, making it impossible for the invaders to harm the body. Still other antibodies stimulate chemical reactions that force the antigens to stick to one another, producing antigen clusters. In turn, the clusters are attacked and eaten by another disease-fighting cell—the macrophage, created in the spleen, liver, and bone marrow. According to physician and science writer Ananya Mandal, "When there is tissue damage or infection, . . . these macrophages can modify themselves to form different structures in order to fight various different microbes and invaders. In this

23

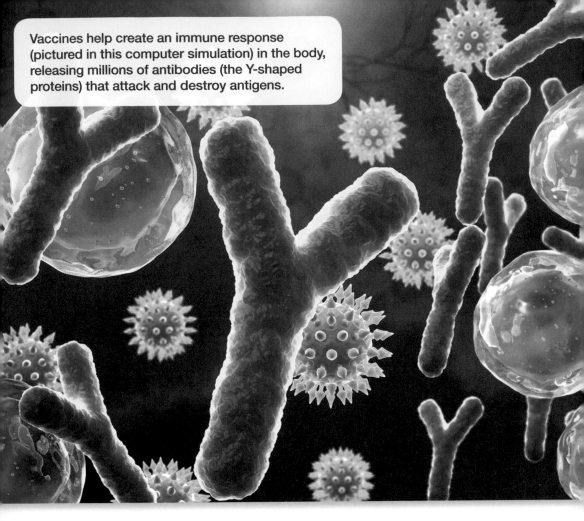

Vaccines help create an immune response (pictured in this computer simulation) in the body, releasing millions of antibodies (the Y-shaped proteins) that attack and destroy antigens.

way, macrophages provide a first line of defence in protecting the host from infection."[14]

Natural Versus Artificial Immunity

The early immunologists not only explained how the immune response works, they also showed how the body acquires immunity to specific disease antigens. First and foremost, the B cells that make antibodies have an innate ability to program themselves to a specific germ or other antigen. That is, once an antigen of a certain disease invades the body, the B cells and antibodies that gather to fight it can later recognize that particular antigen if it happens to appear again. As a result, if the person is infected with that malady a second time, his or her immune system reacts faster than it did the first time. Because the immune cells' second defense is quicker and stronger, it usually rids the body of the infection before it can spread, and the person will not acquire a serious case of the disease. In short, that individual has become immune to the illness in question.

One factor that affects the degree of immunity and how long the protection lasts is the specific nature of the pathogen that attacks the body. One strong immune system reaction to some disease antigens can impart immunity for life. This is the case, for example, with measles, mumps, and yellow fever, each of which is caused by a single antigen. In contrast, a disease like the common cold is caused by hundreds of similar, but in certain ways different, antigens. *New York Times* science writer Jennifer Ackerman explains, "There are more than 200 cold viruses, the most common of which are rhinoviruses (from the Greek "*rin-*," for "nose"). When you encounter a particular strain, your body eventually produces antibodies to it, which remain on hand to quash that virus the next time you're exposed. But with so many flavors of cold virus circulating, there's always a new one to catch."[15] This explains why someone can catch a cold numerous times in the course of his or her life.

When this complex process of gaining immunity occurs on its own, it produces what experts call natural immunity. As Jenner and Pasteur rightly suspected, however, people can also gain immunity in an artificial manner, and that is where vaccines enter the picture. A vaccine sets the immune response against a disease in motion without actually causing that ailment. A clear example is when Pasteur attenuated the germs in his vaccines. The lymphocytes

> "Macrophages provide a first line of defence in protecting the host from infection."[14]
>
> —Physician and science writer Ananya Mandal

> "With so many flavors of cold virus circulating, there's always a new one to catch."[15]
>
> —Science writer Jennifer Ackerman

and macrophages of the people injected with those vaccines easily destroyed those weakened pathogens; yet while this was happening, the attenuated germs stimulated an immune response in which the body's defenses programmed themselves to repel any future infections of that kind.

Development of Killed Vaccines

Even as Ehrlich, Metchnikoff, and others were explaining how natural and artificial immunity work, other researchers were cre-

Immunology's Vital New Tool

A vital tool that twentieth-century immunologists used to learn about microbes and create vaccines to fight them was the electron microscope, introduced by German scientist Ernst Ruska in the 1930s. The instrument employs electrons, which are tiny particles found inside atoms. It allows researchers to see far smaller objects than they can using ordinary optical microscopes. British science writer Chris Woodford compares the workings of the two devices.

> If you've ever used an ordinary microscope, you'll know the basic idea is simple. There's a light at the bottom that shines upward through a thin slice of the specimen. You look through an eyepiece and a powerful lens to see a considerably magnified image of the specimen (typically 10–200 times bigger). . . . [In contrast] in an electron microscope . . . the light source is replaced by a beam of very fast moving electrons. The specimen usually has to be specially prepared and held inside a vacuum chamber from which the air has been pumped out (because electrons do not travel very far in air). The lenses are replaced by a series of coil-shaped magnets through which the electron beam travels. In an ordinary microscope, the glass lenses bend (or refract) the light beams passing through them to produce magnification. In an electron microscope, the coils bend the electron beams the same way. The image is formed as a photograph (called an electron micrograph) or as an image on a TV screen. That's the basic, general idea of an electron microscope.

Chris Woodford, "Electron Microscopes," *Explain That Stuff*, November 23, 2017. www.explainthatstuff.com.

ating new varieties of vaccines. They realized that Pasteur's live attenuated vaccines were quite effective at bringing about long-lasting artificial immunity. Those substances did have one major shortcoming, however; namely, the very fact that the germs in the vaccine were alive. That made them potentially dangerous. Indeed, although the vast majority of people who received those vaccines simply became immune, a small minority did contract those diseases, and a few died. (Evidence has since shown that individuals with impaired immune systems and pregnant women are particularly prone to such reactions to live vaccines.) Pasteur himself was aware of this problem. During his research he wondered whether germs that had been killed with chemicals and thereby rendered harmless might stimulate the desired immune response while having no chance of infecting the host. Other scientists wondered the same thing. In the 1880s two separate teams of medical experts created "killed," or inactivated, vaccines that were reasonably effective in treating swine fever, or hog cholera. (As these names suggest, the disease is deadly to pigs.) Over time, scientists developed a number of killed vaccines for human diseases as well. These included bubonic plague and cholera.

Killed vaccines work, in a sense, by fooling the body's immune system. Jennifer Wright explains this process, as well as an inherent drawback of killed vaccines:

> An inactivated virus can't replicate inside you at all. And amazingly, the immune system still recognizes this inactivated virus as a danger and mounts a response against it. That's great! The downside is that the body doesn't get quite as good at fighting the virus [as it would with a live vaccine]. Killed virus vaccines tend to provide a shorter period of immunity than live virus vaccines, which means at least at first, that they require booster shots every few years.[16]

Toxic Antigens and Toxoid Vaccines

Even as some immunologists were working on usable killed vaccines, other researchers found that germs are not the only kind of dangerous antigen. They discovered that in some diseases the microbes themselves are not harmful; instead, the culprits that injure the body are poisonous secretions the germs produce. Such secretions, called toxins, are the chief antigens of the diseases tetanus, botulism, and diphtheria, for instance.

In fact, diphtheria was the first illness for which scientists created an antitoxin, or toxoid vaccine. According to the World Health Organization (WHO):

> Diphtheria is an infectious disease [that] primarily infects the throat and upper airways, and produces a toxin affecting other organs. The illness has an acute onset and the main characteristics are sore throat, low fever and swollen glands in the neck. . . . The diphtheria toxin causes a membrane of dead tissue to build up over the throat and tonsils, making breathing and swallowing difficult.[17]

Massive outbreaks of diphtheria hit the United States and Europe during the 1800s, killing millions of people, most of them children.

To make a diphtheria vaccine suitable for humans, researchers initially injected guinea pigs with tiny quantities of diphtheria microbes. This caused an immune response to the disease in the animals without causing them to actually catch the disease. The guinea pigs' blood now contained antitoxins that were capable of combating diphtheria toxins. Next the researchers extracted some fluid containing those antitoxins from the creatures' blood and injected it into other lab animals that had not been immunized. Doing this transferred the immunity of the first group of animals into the bodies of animals in the second group. Following this success, the scientists were able to manufacture toxoid vac-

Scientists make diphtheria serum from horse blood. In the late nineteenth century, immunologists discovered they could manufacture toxoid vaccines in animals that could be given to people.

cines in animals that could be given to people. The first of several diphtheria vaccines for humans began to be used in 1892, saving millions of lives globally.

Even more advanced toxoid vaccines emerged during the twentieth century after immunologists managed to treat the toxic antigens with the chemical formalin, which deactivates the toxins. In the same way that killed vaccines pose no risk of infection when injected into the body, deactivated toxins employed in vaccines are largely harmless. Moreover, the deactivated toxins also induce an immune response that generates antibodies programmed to defend against future attacks.

A Large-Scale Assault on Polio

As time went on, the development of effective killed and toxoid vaccines began to strike major blows against several once devastating diseases. So during the first half of the twentieth century, immunologists tried to diversify and perfect these vaccines. The

The Sabin Polio Vaccine

The earliest polio vaccine was a killed vaccine developed by Jonas Salk in the early 1950s. Although it successfully created immunity to the disease, it required boosters to maintain immunity. The potential danger this posed was that some people might, for one reason or another, fail to get their boosters. That would leave them open to coming down with polio at some future date. For this reason, other immunologists continued to search for a live attenuated polio vaccine that would provide long-lasting immunity.

Success came in 1963 with the release of a vaccine developed by Dr. Albert B. Sabin of the University of Cincinnati College of Medicine. Unlike earlier attempts at producing a live attenuated polio vaccine, the Sabin vaccine caused those injected with it no harmful effects. In fact, the vaccine proved to have some advantages over the Salk vaccine. One was that the live viruses used in the Sabin vaccine induced a stronger immune response and imparted long-lasting immunity. Also, Sabin's vaccine can be taken orally, making it easier and less painful to administer. Together, the Salk and Sabin vaccines produced an astonishing global preventative effect. By 1969 polio had almost disappeared in the United States, Canada, Europe, and Asia.

hope was that they would continue to make headway against all kinds of pathogens, including the smallest of all germs—viruses.

The era's most spectacular success in the fight against viruses—as well as one of history's most extraordinary medical advances—was the development of vaccines to prevent poliomyelitis, or polio for short. That disease, also called infantile paralysis, usually paralyzes its victims to one degree or another. It most often attacks children younger than fourteen, although adults can also contract it. More than twenty-seven thousand people came down with polio in the United States alone in 1916, and of these some six thousand died. The number of cases increased thereafter, and by the 1940s there were more than forty thousand reported cases in some years. One noted medical authority of that period remarked, "There is literally no acute disease at the present day which causes so much apprehension and alarm in the patient and his relatives."[18]

Indeed, the fact that polio struck so many young people inspired scientists to mount a particularly large-scale assault on it. To help raise money for that effort, in 1938 President Franklin D. Roosevelt established a huge charitable campaign, the National Foundation for Infantile Paralysis, which later was renamed the March of Dimes. Roosevelt, who was first elected to the presidency in 1932, had a special interest in the disease—he himself had been struck by polio in 1921. The onrush of muscle failures on the day he first felt sick illustrates the frightening speed at which polio can overtake a victim. According to his online biography at the FDR 4 Freedoms Project, "The first morning after his symptoms appeared, FDR's left leg nearly buckled beneath him as he tried to rise from bed. By that night, his right leg also was losing strength, and he could hardly stand. The day after that, a Friday, he couldn't stand, nor move his legs or even sit up, and terrible pain wracked his neck and back."[19]

Hoping to spare as many people as possible from such agonies, large teams of researchers worked around the clock for several years. At first they tried attenuating the live polio germs, reasoning this would make the virus stimulate an immune response without causing the disease. But when they tested this initial vaccine on several thousand children, a few contracted polio and died. The scientists immediately withdrew that vaccine and tried to discover what had gone wrong. First, they found, the chemicals they had used to attenuate the germs had not weakened them all; a few remained full strength and dangerous. Moreover, the researchers had wrongly assumed that polio is caused by a single virus. In reality, they learned, there are more than one hundred distinct polio viruses, and a vaccine that protects against one may not protect against the others.

Salk's Triumph

This disappointing discovery made progress in the fight against polio slow and painstaking for a while. Then, in 1948, the National

Foundation for Infantile Paralysis hired a young researcher named Jonas Salk to tackle the disease. Salk carefully studied the various polio strains while gathering a team of more than fifty experts in immunology, biology, and chemistry. They decided that a killed vaccine that would work against all the polio strains was the most realistic, as well as the safest, approach. Eventually, they settled on the chemical formaldehyde as the killing agent, after which they conducted extensive tests of the resulting vaccine on monkeys.

Dr. Jonas Salk administers a polio vaccine. Mass polio vaccinations of children began in 1954, and by 1961 only five hundred cases of polio were reported in the United States.

By mid-1953 Salk felt he was ready to administer the vaccine to humans. Before doing so on a large scale, he courageously tested it on himself and the members of his immediate family. When these trials proved successful, he told the foundation it was time to move forward with mass vaccinations of children, which began in April 1954. More than 1.8 million children aged six to nine received injections.

Thereafter, a large evaluation team led by Dr. Thomas Francis of the University of Michigan vigilantly monitored the results of what newspapers dubbed the greatest mass test of a scientific discovery in history. After a full year of study, Francis made even bigger headlines

> "Vaccines against diphtheria, polio, and whooping cough hammered these childhood killers."[20]
>
> —Physician Meredith Wadman

when he announced that Salk's vaccine was a triumph. It was both successful and safe. As a result, mass production of it, along with large-scale vaccinations around the globe, quickly followed. Incredibly, in 1961, only six years after the vaccine's approval, US medical authorities reported a mere five hundred cases of polio— less than 1 percent of the annual number in the early 1950s.

The progress made by vaccines against other terrible diseases in the same period were no less dramatic. Physician and science writer Meredith Wadman writes, "During World War II and the two decades following it, childhood mortality declined strikingly, in large part because of dramatic inroads against infectious diseases." This happened, she goes on, because "vaccines against diphtheria, polio, and whooping cough hammered these childhood killers." What she calls "a heroic quest" by researchers who were "driven and well-funded"[20] had made the world far safer from the ravages of disease than it had ever been.

CHAPTER 3

Triumph over a Host of Deadly Maladies

From the mid-twentieth century to the early 2000s, immunologists worked with and perfected a range of different types of vaccines. As happened in the early 1900s, each new one showed success, to one degree or another, in fighting a disease that once afflicted humanity, killing untold numbers of people in each decade.

Yet after the 1960s the general approach to vaccine production changed. Before, scientists had been intent on developing new vaccines as fast as possible in order to eradicate polio and certain other rampant child-killing maladies. In contrast, they now began to take whatever time was necessary to develop new *kinds* of vaccines, in each case ensuring that they were as safe as possible to administer. Physician Kristen A. Feemster explains, "Amid widespread availability of vaccines, the occurrence of vaccine-preventable diseases decreased, and urgency was no longer the primary driver. Vaccine development placed greater emphasis on *benefit over risk*. [There was] as much emphasis on how safe a vaccine is for healthy people as on a vaccine's capacity to prevent disease."[21]

Also driving vaccine research from the 1960s and 1970s on were new discoveries relating to the human body's cells and the chemical processes that happen inside them. Some scientists looked at the physical properties of various dangerous pathogens and how these microbes trigger antibody production. Other researchers studied the biological processes that guide heredity, the passing on of physical traits from parents to children through the genetic code known as deoxyribonucleic acid (DNA). This brought about the creation of ingenious new vaccines that use elements of that code to heal or immunize people.

Subunit and DNA Vaccines

Those so-called DNA vaccines, which modern immunologists continue to study and develop, are one variety of a larger group called subunit vaccines. As the name suggests, such a vaccine utilizes not an entire germ but rather only a small section or particle of that microbe. To actually contract a given disease, a person needs to be invaded by the whole germ. The advantage of a subunit vaccine is that the small piece of the pathogen that is injected into a patient cannot cause the disease, yet it does stimulate the desired immune response.

Diverse subunit vaccines can be made from differing pieces of a microbe. Among those possible subunits are genes, the tiny particles that are located within cells and carry individual pieces of hereditary information. Scientists who specialize in dealing with genes, the genetic code, and DNA are called genetic engineers. Genetic engineering sprang from scientists James Watson's and Francis Crick's 1953 discovery of the structure of the DNA molecule. This big, highly complex cluster of atoms, bearing a spiral shape, is the primary element of genes and contains the genetic code that determines the numerous traits that parents pass on to their children.

The significance of DNA studies to the field of immunology was nothing less than immense. In part, this is because microbes have DNA and genes, just like animals and people. This fact allowed scientists to single out one or more individual genes within the DNA of targeted disease germs. Such a gene, which becomes the subunit in a subunit vaccine, contains so-called messenger chemicals that tell the body to form germ-fighting antibodies. At the same time, the gene by itself cannot cause the person who receives the vaccine to contract the disease in question.

To create a DNA vaccine based on a gene from a specific microbe, researchers learned to separate that gene, which bears the messenger chemicals, from the germ itself. Next they injected the gene, constituting the subunit, into completely harmless germs they had cultured in the lab. Among the more common safe, cultured germs used to make subunit vaccines are baker's yeasts. Once the gene from the target disease had joined with the harmless cultured germs—forming a tailored microbe,

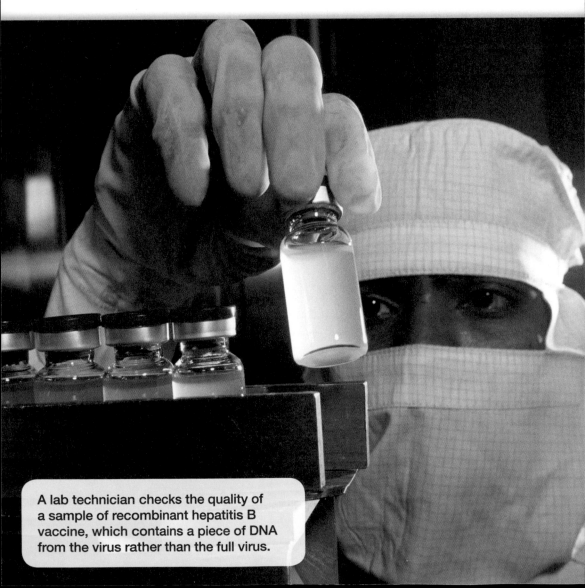

A lab technician checks the quality of a sample of recombinant hepatitis B vaccine, which contains a piece of DNA from the virus rather than the full virus.

or cell—the scientists could grow enough of the new cells to make a vaccine. The National Institutes of Health explains the safety and usefulness of such vaccines in the following way: "The DNA vaccine [cannot] cause the disease because it [does not] contain the microbe, just copies of a few of its genes. In addition, DNA vaccines are relatively easy and inexpensive to design and produce."[22]

Because subunit vaccines are made by combining or recombining DNA from two different living organisms, scientists often refer to this technique as recombinant DNA technology. The first widely successful subunit vaccine was the Merck Sharpe and Dohme vaccine for hepatitis B, which the US Food and Drug Administration approved for use in 1986. (Hepatitis B is a debilitating ailment that affects the liver and blood; it is frequently contracted from infected blood during blood transfusions.) That vaccine was so effective that medical authorities in numerous parts of the world approved its use for young children as a preventative—a tactic designed to keep a person from catching a particular disease in the first place.

> "The DNA vaccine [cannot] cause the disease because it [does not] contain the microbe, just copies of a few of its genes."[22]
>
> —National Institutes of Health

Combating Influenza and Pertussis

Other illnesses for which immunologists developed or are at present developing subunit vaccines include measles, Lyme disease, AIDS, and influenza. The latter, more commonly known as the flu, kills several thousand people every year. Its victims live in all nations, including the United States, partly because the disease has hundreds of strains and also because it is very contagious and spreads easily and quickly. The flu outbreak in the winter of 2017–2018 was worse than most in the preceding few decades. Yet even the most damaging modern outbreaks pale in comparison to those of the early 1900s. From 1918 to 1919, for instance, influenza caused more than 20 million deaths globally. At least 550,000 Americans died—ten times more than the country lost in World War I.

The potential for another flu epidemic of massive proportions still looms because the viruses that cause the illness can mutate, becoming new strains, at any time. Most new strains tend to be more or less similar to the others, yet a very dangerous one that is resistant to existing vaccines is an ever-present possibility. For these reasons, influenza has long been and continues to be a major target for immunologists. They developed several different flu vaccines in the late 1900s and early 2000s. Some of these were made from killed germs. Another is a subunit version that separates a protein from the flu virus and combines it with harmless cultured substances.

Another sometimes fatal disease that is treated with subunit vaccines is pertussis, better known as whooping cough. It is an extremely contagious malady caused by a bacterium. Someone who contracts whooping cough typically starts out with cold- or flu-like symptoms, including a runny nose. Because it can seem to be merely a common cold, people who contract it may be completely unaware they are spreading it to others. Eventually, affected individuals develop a cough, which can become so violent that they can vomit or even suffer broken ribs. In contrast, infants often display little or no coughing and instead suddenly stop breathing for several seconds or longer.

Left untreated, pertussis can lead to death; it used to claim large numbers of victims worldwide each year. Before scientists engineered vaccines to fight it in the 1940s, whooping cough killed about nine thousand people in the United States alone each year. Today that number stands at fewer than twenty per year.

The first pertussis vaccine was made from whole germs that had been inactivated. Although it did save millions of lives over time, it had a number of unwanted side effects. So immunologists developed a subunit vaccine to fight the disease. It uses indi-

A Sexually Transmitted Disease with Unusual Ease of Transmission

The HPV virus is so widespread that at a minimum, according to the Population Reference Bureau, at least 75 percent of sexually active men and women are exposed to it at some point. Evidence suggests that in a majority of cases, HPV shows few or no symptoms and disappears on its own after a few months or so. The problem is that during the interval in which someone carries the virus, she or he can and often does pass it on to one or more sexual partners. Some of those individuals will become infected. As a result of this ease of transmission, an estimated 20 million or more Americans, making up almost 7 percent of the US population, are infected with HPV at any given time. Also, exposure to the virus can lead to more serious problems down the road. Some strains of HPV can cause genital warts or cancer of the cervix, penis, anus, or throat.

vidual pieces of the pertussis bacterium that stimulate an immune response in the body without causing the disease. (The subunit version is today administered in combination with the toxoid vaccines for diphtheria and tetanus.)

An Extremely Widespread Infection

Still another germ-driven illness that immunologists targeted in the late 1900s and early 2000s is a sexually transmitted disease, known as human papilloma virus (HPV). HPV is not a single virus. Instead, it includes over one hundred separate but very similar viruses that infect the skin, usually (though not always) around the genitals.

HPV, which can also be transmitted in nonsexual ways, is extremely widespread around the globe, including the United States. According to the US Department of Health and Human Services, "HPV infections are so common that nearly all men and women get at least 1 type of HPV at some point in their lives; and the complications can be serious. About 17,500 women and 9,300 men get cancer caused by HPV infections in the United States every year. Many of these cancers don't cause symptoms until they've gotten serious and hard to treat."[23]

In the 1980s German researchers discovered HPV viruses in women's genital tumors, and in the 1990s the National Cancer Institute launched two large-scale studies of HPV. Initial steps toward developing an effective vaccine were taken in the same de-

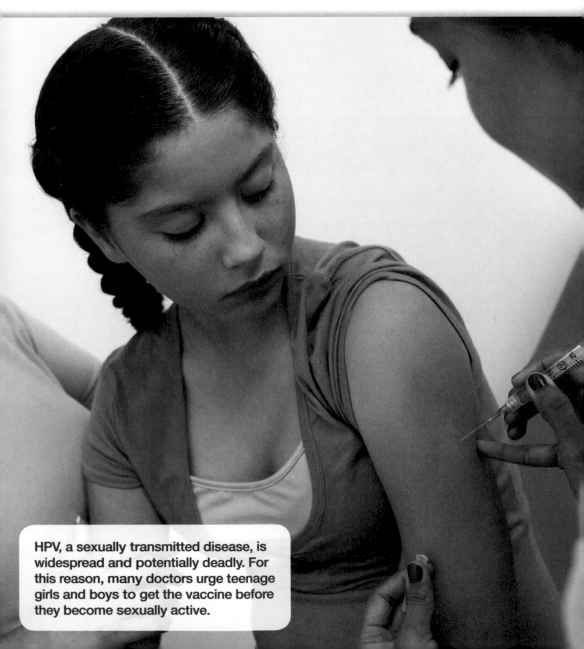

HPV, a sexually transmitted disease, is widespread and potentially deadly. For this reason, many doctors urge teenage girls and boys to get the vaccine before they become sexually active.

cade. The first of those vaccines, called Gardasil, was released by Merck in 2006. The following year, another major pharmaceutical company, GlaxoSmithKline, introduced its own HPV vaccine called Cervarix.

Both vaccines are subunit types, made from proteins found on the outer layers of the most common HPV viruses. Because the proteins are only small pieces of those germs, people vaccinated with them cannot contract the disease from the injections. At the same time, when the body's immune system detects the proteins, it reacts as if they *are* full-fledged viruses and vigorously attacks them. In addition, the vaccinated person gains immunity to those HPV germs.

> "HPV infections are so common that nearly all men and women get at least 1 type of HPV at some point in their lives."[23]
>
> —US Department of Health and Human Services

Malaria—Getting Around a Unique Roadblock

Even as subunit vaccines were under development in the second half of the twentieth century, immunologists worked on a sort of parallel line of vaccines collectively known as synthetic peptides. Like the ordinary subunit variety, synthetic peptides fool the body into thinking that a disease germ is invading and thus stimulate the production of antibodies. The difference is in the word *synthetic*, which means "artificial." First the lab technicians locate the part of a germ's surface that triggers the body's immune response. In several types of microbes, this tiny subunit is a peptide (hence the second half of the name of this kind of vaccine), which is a building block of a protein.

After isolating the peptide, the technicians synthesize, or create from scratch, an exact copy of it using various chemicals. Later, when a doctor injects the synthetic peptide into a person's body, the cells of his or her immune system react as if it came from a germ. An immune response begins, and because the germ is not used, there is zero risk of catching the disease.

Synthetic peptides have shown considerable promise for fighting diseases caused by large parasites called protozoa. Those illnesses include, among several others, Chagas' disease, leishmaniasis, sleeping sickness (trypanosomiasis), and the most widespread of the group, malaria. Transmitted mostly by mosquitoes, malaria causes high fever, chills, and sometimes death. In 2016 WHO reported about 216 million cases of malaria, most of them in poor developing nations. Of those cases, some 445,000 resulted in death.

While many of the malaria vaccines developed in recent years are synthetic, one notable one is not. From 2012 to 2016 a new malaria vaccine that employs live parasites underwent initial trials to test its effectiveness, first on animals and then on humans. Earlier attempts to create effective vaccines against malaria—going back several decades—ran into a roadblock unique to protozoan infections. Namely, once these parasites have invaded a body, they can mutate multiple times over the course of months, thereby changing their form. Each change can trigger a new infection that is often resistant to a vaccine that worked on the microbe's initial form. According to Stephen Hoffman, former director of malaria research at the Naval Medical Research Institute in Bethesda, Maryland, and the key developer of the new vaccine, this makes malaria much harder to fight than bacterial and viral diseases.

> "I'm envisioning total success."[24]
>
> —Noted immunologist Stephen Hoffman on the possible effectiveness of his malaria vaccine

To get around the difficulties caused by protozoan mutations, the new vaccine uses a novel approach. Hoffman and his colleagues snared a number of malaria-carrying mosquitoes and dosed them with enough radiation to severely weaken the parasites but not enough to kill either them or the insects. Then, using a powerful microscope, the researchers harvested thousands of the irradiated protozoans from the mosquitoes'

A hospital worker in Liberia screens blood samples for malaria. The WHO reported 216 million cases of malaria in 2016, most of them in poor developing nations.

salivary glands. The vaccine made from the live but weakened germs gave all of the initial test subjects—nonhuman and human alike—immunity to malaria. When asked for a prediction of how the vaccine would work on large populations, Hoffman confidently responded, "I'm envisioning total success."[24]

Measles, Mumps, and More

During the years that Hoffman and his colleagues were struggling to develop an effective live malaria vaccine, other immunologists worked to perfect various other live attenuated vaccines. One of the most widely used and effective was the first one designed to fight measles. The US Department of Health and Human Services website says of the disease, "Measles is one of the most contagious diseases there is. If 1 person has it, 9 out of 10 people close to that person who aren't immune (protected) will also get measles. And it can be dangerous. Serious cases of measles can lead to brain damage and even death."[25]

Social and Economic Benefits of Vaccines

Vaccines do more than simply protect people from harmful diseases. WHO explains how vaccines also empower women, stimulate economic growth, and promote equity among different socioeconomic groups.

For example, thanks to vaccines, far fewer babies die in various societies than died before the advent of vaccines. As a result, many women in those societies decide to have fewer children, since they know that most of the infants they do have will eventually reach adulthood. Vaccines also benefit society in other ways, including by promoting economic growth. This happens because with vaccines, fewer people get sick. That means far fewer lost workdays, which increases productivity and profits at all sorts of companies. The annual return on investment in vaccination—that is, the amount a society saves by investing a relatively small amount in vaccination programs—is estimated to be somewhere between 12 percent and 18 percent, which in an average national economy amounts to billions of dollars saved. "The benefits of vaccination," WHO states, "extend beyond prevention of specific diseases in individuals. They enable a rich, multifaceted harvest for societies and nations. Vaccination makes good economic sense, and meets the need to care for the weakest members of societies."

F.E. Andre et al., "Vaccination Greatly Reduces Disease, Disability, Death and Inequity Worldwide," World Health Organization, 2018. www.who.int.

In 1971 scientists unveiled the so-called MMR vaccine, which protects against not only measles but also two other common childhood maladies: mumps and rubella (often called the German measles). Thereafter, the vaccine, which uses weakened live measles germs, was routinely given to small children. Almost immediately, the number of reported cases of measles in the United States fell dramatically, from hundreds of thousands per year to a few thousand per year. Moreover, further reductions in measles infections took place over time. From 1997 to 2013, for example, fewer than 200 cases of the disease occurred per year in the United States. At the same time, reported cases of mumps fell from more than 150,000 per year in the late 1960s to fewer than 300 per year by 2001.

A second live attenuated measles vaccine, dubbed MMRV, was approved by the US Food and Drug Administration in 2005. It is similar to MMR, but it adds protection for a fourth disease that frequently strikes children—varicella, or chicken pox.

These four contagions represent only a small fraction of the host of deadly maladies over which vaccines have allowed modern medicine to triumph. Diseases either eradicated or reduced to a mere handful of cases per year include smallpox, diphtheria, whooping cough, tetanus, pneumococcal diseases, hepatitis A and B, and polio, to name only a few. A 2017 study headed by S. Jay Olshansky, professor of epidemiology at the University of Chicago School of Public Health, found that from 1963 to 2015, vaccines prevented some 4.5 billion cases of disease and saved more than 10 million lives. As WHO puts it, providing "universal access to safe vaccines [allows] every individual to have the opportunity to live a healthier and fuller life."[26]

CHAPTER 4

A Modern Backlash Against Vaccination

Up until the late 1990s, the vast majority of American parents made sure to go along with their doctors' recommendations to vaccinate their children against measles, mumps, diphtheria, and numerous other dangerous diseases. But that mind-set suddenly changed in the years that followed. Surveys showed that doctors themselves encountered shifting attitudes among parents. In 2006 roughly 75 percent of pediatricians reported having at least one parent of a patient refuse to allow that child to be vaccinated. By 2013, 87 percent of pediatricians said the same thing. Also from 2006 to 2013, the surveys indicated, the average number of parents who rejected vaccines for their children increased from close to zero to 3.3 percent. That percentage represented more than 2 million families.

Claims and Counterclaims

In that same period, some parents in that group spoke publicly about their decision to avoid vaccination. The reasons given by these so-called anti-vaxxers varied. Some claimed that vaccines were unnecessary; others said they feared that various additives, including preservatives, in vaccines might be harmful; and still others suggested that vaccines might cause debilitating conditions, including autism. (A person with autism tends to have diminished social and interpersonal communication skills and displays certain repetitive behaviors.)

In 2007, for example, in a broadcast of *The Oprah Winfrey Show*, popular actress Jenny McCarthy said she believed that vaccines had caused her son's autism. Such statements by celebrities had a measurable impact on a number of parents across the country. "It was enough to scare any mother,"[27] commented Eileen Pike of West Palm Beach, Florida, who decided to delay vaccination for her own young son.

Immunologists forcefully pushed back against these beliefs and public statements. By refusing to vaccinate their children, they explained, anti-vaxxers were putting society as a whole at risk. This, they went on, is because vaccines protect not only individuals but also those around them, a phenomenon called herd immunity. In the words of one expert observer, "In order for a community to be fully protected against a disease, 80 to 90 percent of its population needs to have been vaccinated." If the coverage falls below that level, the expert explains, "a school, a

Anti-vaxxers in California rally against mandatory vaccinations for schoolchildren. Many argue that vaccinations are unnecessary or harmful and may cause autism and other debilitating conditions.

"It is imperative that we are well-informed before making a decision about vaccination."[29]

—Physician Kristen A. Feemster

church, or a neighborhood becomes susceptible to the disease. Babies who aren't old enough to get the shot yet are at the greatest risk of becoming sick."[28]

In contrast to these claims and counterclaims, some concerned experts have tried not to take sides. Understanding that there could be legitimate reasons why some parents might question vaccinating their children, they have called on those on both sides of the issue to thoroughly educate themselves about the advantages and disadvantages of vaccination before making a decision about their use. Physician Kristen A. Feemster, for example, advises:

> It is imperative that we are well-informed before making a decision about vaccination. This requires an understanding of (1) how vaccines work, (2) the diseases that vaccines prevent, and (3) why vaccines are important to individuals and society. Vaccines and their role in society represent a complex interplay between sociopolitical systems, culture, economics, individual beliefs, and health literacy—and with that, they provide a multitude of fronts for the introduction of conflicting messages or incorrect information.[29]

A Link Between Vaccines and Autism?

Most of this modern controversy about possible harmful effects of vaccination, including claims that vaccines might cause autism, began with the appearance of a scientific paper in 1998. A group of British researchers led by Dr. Andrew Wakefield published the study in the highly respected medical journal the *Lancet*. The paper claimed that people who had been vaccinated with the MMR vaccine had increased risk of developing a disease of the bowel (intestines).

In a second study connected to the first one, Wakefield said that he had found evidence that the bowel condition could lead to autism. So he believed there might be some kind of link between vaccines and autism. Furthermore, Wakefield followed up the paper with the release of a video. In it, he went so far as to say that the MMR vaccine actually caused autism.

The immediate reactions in Britain, the United States, and elsewhere to Wakefield's 1998 paper and video were loud and

A Mother's Fears

This excerpt is from an online blog post titled "How I Became Anti-vaccine." The author, who does not list her name and claims to be a toxicologist, briefly recalls some of the reasons why she became convinced that vaccines can lead to harmful effects in children.

I chose a delayed and selective vaccine schedule for my son. I was torn between the risk of a "preventable" disease and the risk of vaccine injury. I didn't know as much as I do now.

The first time he received vaccines, at 4 months of age, he was somnolent [drowsy] for 4 hrs following the shot, awake but out of it. I was worried, because it wasn't like him to be awake and not fully alert, but I felt some relief when he seemed to be back to himself later that day. . . .

Three days after [receiving a] second set of vaccines, my son started showing signs of having neurological damage—he developed some kind of head tic, which looking back, appears to have potentially been non-febrile seizures (no fever). I didn't connect it to the vaccines at the time. I didn't know that [some vaccines] contain aluminum. I didn't know that aluminum has been linked to tics in scientific studies. . . . But I know now.

I was still naive, ignorant, and fearful of diseases for the next year of my son's life. I was caught in between the risks of the diseases and the risks of the vaccines.

Think, Love, Healthy (blog), "How I Became Anti-vaccine," August 1, 2016. https://thinklovehealthy.com.

opinionated. On one side were untold numbers of parents who knew little or nothing about how vaccines work and had heard that some scientists had linked vaccines to autism. For at least some of these parents, doubts about the safety of vaccines had been firmly implanted in their minds.

Moreover, in the years that followed, some members of the next generation of parents inherited those doubts. As late as 2017, *Parents* magazine's online edition reported on the thoughts of people like Grand Forks, North Dakota, resident Lisa Estall, who took her young daughter Summer to the doctor to be vaccinated. Although Summer did receive the injection, her mother told the reporters how nervous she was about it because of what she had heard. "Everywhere I go," she said, "someone's talking about the danger of vaccines. There are moms posting about their kids' side effects on just about every online parenting forum. The other day I had coffee with two friends, and one of them said she wasn't vaccinating her kids. I can't help but wonder: Should I really be injecting a healthy child with these things?"[30]

> "Should I really be injecting a healthy child with these things?"[30]
>
> —North Dakota mother Lisa Estall on whether to vaccinate her child

The Medical Establishment Reacts

The chief reaction from the other side of the developing debate on vaccine safety—composed of immunologists, physicians, and health officials—was extreme concern over Wakefield's and his colleagues' accusations. Members of the medical establishment were initially worried for two reasons. First, what if the 1998 paper's authors were right? If further studies showed that they were indeed correct—that a vaccine could cause autism—it was a grave matter, and vaccine use would need to be seriously reevaluated. Second, and conversely, if Wakefield was proved wrong, he would have frightened many parents into abandoning vaccination. That would be hugely problematic because, as a result, many people would contract deadly diseases who would not have if they had been vaccinated.

Wakefield's claim, based on a study of a mere twelve cases, was that the MMR vaccine had caused bowel inflammation. That, he suggested, induced brain-damaging proteins to circulate through the patients' bodies, and that had led to autism. Hearing that claim, medical researchers in labs around the world geared up to do their scientific duty. In science, for any new discovery or claim to be considered valid and thereafter accepted by all scientists, it must be repeatable and provable in subsequent studies by unbiased researchers. If many studies produce the same results and thereby corroborate the discovery, it becomes widely accepted; but if no other studies end up producing the same results, the discovery is viewed as a fluke or frivolous and is rejected.

This classic process of the scientific method proceeded in the aftermath of the Wakefield paper's publication. Numerous carefully administered studies were done in dozens of research facilities

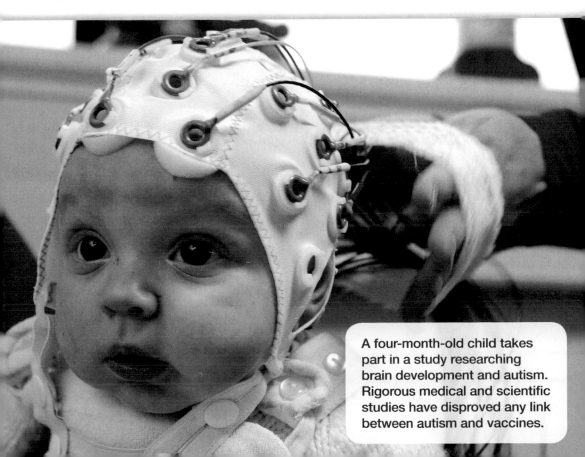

A four-month-old child takes part in a study researching brain development and autism. Rigorous medical and scientific studies have disproved any link between autism and vaccines.

in several countries—all searching for the supposed link between the MMR vaccine and autism—or for that matter, *any* ill effects of that vaccine. Yet the incidence of bowel inflammation and resulting autism was never demonstrated. Not a single research team was able to find the claimed link between the two conditions, nor did researchers uncover any other previously unknown negative effects.

Moreover, Feemster points out that this inability of Wakefield's findings to be repeated was a major embarrassment to the distinguished journal that had reviewed and published those findings. "In 2010, the *Lancet* took the extraordinary step of retracting the paper, with the journal's editor-in-chief [stating that its] editorial board had been 'deceived' by the authors' representation of their methods."[31]

In addition, various scientists subsequently found flaws in Wakefield's research, as well as ethics violations in the manner in which he presented his findings. This led to public rebukes of Wakefield and the claims about autism he had put forth in the paper. Such censures of a researcher by the scientific community as a whole have rarely been seen in the annals of modern science, Feemster explains. "Wakefield lost his medical license due to the fraudulent claims put forth in his article. Since that time, multiple rigorous studies comparing vaccinated to unvaccinated children have not shown an increased risk for autism after vaccination."[32]

Falling Vaccination Rates Around the Globe

In spite of most immunologists' and other scientists' insistence that no link exists between vaccines and autism, some parents continued to refuse to allow their children to be vaccinated. In 1997, the year before Wakefield's paper was published, measles vaccination rates in Britain were higher than 91 percent; in comparison, in late 1998, shortly after the paper's appearance, those rates began to fall. They reached 80 percent in the winter

Raising the Money to Make Compensation

One of the more common questions that people unfamiliar with the National Vaccine Injury Compensation Program ask is where the money for the compensated parties comes from. The program's website provides the answer to that question, explaining:

> The Vaccine Injury Compensation Trust Fund provides funding for the National Vaccine Injury Compensation Program to compensate vaccine-related injury or death petitions for covered vaccines administered on or after October 1, 1988.
>
> Funded by a $.75 excise tax on vaccines recommended by the Centers for Disease Control and Prevention for routine administration to children, the excise tax is imposed on each dose (i.e., disease that is prevented) of a vaccine. Trivalent influenza vaccine for example, is taxed $.75 because it prevents one disease; measles-mumps-rubella vaccine, which prevents three diseases, is taxed $2.25.
>
> The Department of Treasury collects the excise taxes and manages the Fund's investments and produces Vaccine Injury Compensation Trust Fund Monthly Reports [that are available online for the public to read].

Health Resources & Human Services Administration, "About the National Vaccine Injury Compensation Program," 2017. www.hrsa.gov.

of 2003–2004 and were even lower in specific areas of the British Isles. Similar drops in vaccination rates occurred in the United States and some other countries in the same period.

As a result of the decreases in vaccination rates, all of these nations experienced minor but troubling outbreaks of diseases that vaccines had earlier nearly eradicated. In only the first two months of 2014, for example, fifty-four cases of measles were reported in the United States; this was an unusually high figure, considering that in the years immediately prior to the 1998

Wakefield paper, only about sixty measles cases occurred each year. There were also increases in the incidence of whooping cough, mumps, and some other ailments normally kept in check by vaccines.

In Continental Europe, meanwhile, such outbreaks were often much larger. In 2014 there were more than twelve thousand confirmed cases of measles, some thirty-three hundred of them in a single country (Italy). Overall, Europe's measles outbreak resulted in thirty-five deaths, mostly of children, thirty-one of which happened in Romania alone. According to WHO, in 2014 and 2015 only 88 percent of Romanian children were vaccinated, down from a high of 97 percent years before. Local medical authorities attributed most of the drop in vaccination rates to parents refusing to vaccinate their children out of fear that vaccines might be unsafe.

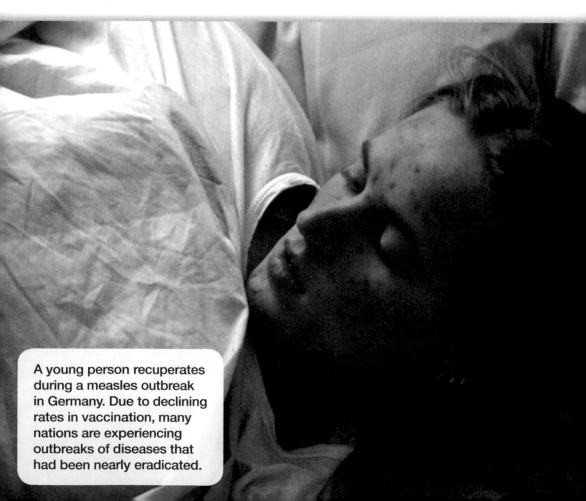

A young person recuperates during a measles outbreak in Germany. Due to declining rates in vaccination, many nations are experiencing outbreaks of diseases that had been nearly eradicated.

Vaccine Side Effects and Drawbacks

Although vaccination rates tend to go up and down slightly from year to year in various nations, the overall trend of lower-than-normal vaccination rates has continued to the present. In the United States ongoing fear of vaccination by some parents is not based only on the supposed link between vaccines and autism. Anti-vaxxers cite a number of other worries about what vaccination might do to their children.

For example, there is a fair amount of concern about the very real side effects of vaccination, the existence of which scientists fully admit. One such side effect is a type of seizure (a momentary episode in which the body convulses) known as a febrile seizure. Such episodes can happen to any young child who has a moderately high fever. In fact, about one in every twenty young people will have a febrile seizure at some point in his or her childhood. Vaccination can sometimes cause a fever. Therefore, the procedure automatically raises the risk of febrile and other kinds of seizures. An estimated one in ten thousand vaccinations cause such an episode.

Another, and more dangerous, possible side effect of receiving a vaccine is anaphylaxis, a severe allergic reaction that can cause extreme discomfort and, when left untreated, death. If a patient has an allergy to an ingredient in a vaccine, she or he can have an anaphylactic reaction. About one in every million vaccinations results in that sort of reaction. (Almost always, however, the doctor administering the vaccine will have the proper device—an EpiPen—on hand to treat it.)

Still other adverse side effects of vaccination are possible, though rare. One is a form of eczema, a skin infection caused by the so-called vaccinia virus. Most of the few people who get it already have a history of rashes and infections of the skin. Even rarer is a progressive infection of the vaccinia virus, which can be fatal. It occurs when a vaccination site fails to heal normally, allowing the virus to spread. Another skin infection—Stevens-Johnson syndrome—normally occurs in drug users but can on occasion be associated with vaccination. Experts estimate that it occurs in about three cases for every million vaccinations.

A less worrisome side effect of vaccination is fainting. A few children who are particularly anxious about the injection can experience a sudden rise in heart rate and blood pressure, leading to a brief loss of consciousness. (This phenomenon is not exclusive to vaccine injections; for *any* type of injection, a small percentage of children who fear the stick of a needle do faint.)

Some parents also worry that a vaccine will cause their children to contract the very disease the vaccine is meant to protect against. However, as the Centers for Disease Control and Prevention says, that scenario occurs

> "A vaccine causing full-blown disease would be extremely unlikely."[33]
>
> —Centers for Disease Control and Prevention

almost never. With an inactivated (killed) vaccine, it isn't possible. Dead viruses or bacteria can't cause disease. With live vaccines, some children get what appears to be a mild case of disease (for example, what looks like a measles or chickenpox rash, but with only a few spots). This isn't harmful, and can actually show that the vaccine is working. A vaccine causing full-blown disease would be extremely unlikely.[33]

Fears on Both Sides

For some or all of these reasons, a small proportion of parents in the United States and several other countries say they do not want to take the chance that their children might experience adverse reactions to vaccination. Scientists say that the risks and drawbacks associated with vaccines are relatively tiny. They argue that with rare exceptions, the benefits of vaccines outweigh the very small health risks those injections pose.

In response, some anti-vaxxers argue the opposite—that in their eyes, the supposed benefits of vaccines do not outweigh the health risks, even though those risks may be small. For example, a mother may hear that without the vaccine, there is a one in a million chance her child will get polio. She may also be told that if the child is vaccinated he or she has one chance in five hundred thousand of having a serious seizure. From this point of view, the chances of having the seizure are greater than those of contracting polio, so the mother may decide against vaccination and take the smaller risk of her child getting polio.

For those few parents who *have* taken the risk of vaccination and found that their children did experience adverse side effects, there is some recourse. It consists of the National Vaccine Injury Compensation Program, created in 1988. In some ways like a judge and jury in a court, it hears cases about injuries caused by vaccination. A US Department of Health and Human Services medical staff reviews a claim, and the US Department of Justice looks at the staff's medical recommendation and submits it to a court. The latter may grant monetary compensation to the injured party.

In the long run, whichever side in the vaccine safety debate is right, both sides have more in common than they may realize. As physician and expert on children's health Chris Spinelli states, "Remember that ultimately the argument both for and against vaccines is one of fear, the fear of what might happen." He adds:

> The prime argument *against* vaccination plays on parents' fears that their child will have some chronic developmental damage and not be normal due to the vaccines. The argument *for* vaccination is based on the fear of infectious diseases that we have seen cause either death or severe, chronic developmental and neurological damage to children and adults around the world.[34]

Clearly, each side sees its fears as more significant than those of the other side. As a result, the debate continues.

CHAPTER 5

New Research and the Future of Vaccines

Large amounts of money, time, and technological resources at present pour into research on new as well as older vaccines. Immunologists and the governments around the world that fund and support them continually keep in mind vaccines' enormous past successes. Vaccination has clearly saved untold millions of lives globally since the start of the twentieth century. Seeking to build on those achievements, researchers are hard at work in labs in the United States, Britain, Canada, Denmark, Germany, China, South Korea, and numerous other countries.

All of these scientists are trying to overcome some major challenges. One is that despite vaccination's past accomplishments, no vaccines yet exist for several debilitating diseases. In part this is because some of the poorer countries and regions of the world have little or no infrastructures (clinics, research programs, necessary staffs, and so forth) for large-scale vaccination programs. So local diseases that affect only those regions tend not to be high on scientists' lists of maladies requiring immediate vaccine research. Another challenge is that creating a new vaccine is costly. To make the costs involved worth it, companies that produce vaccines try to market them everywhere they can. But even when discounted, the cost of vaccines is sometimes too high for the most impoverished nations. New ways to keep production costs down are therefore needed. In addition, although many of the current vaccines are highly effective, the medical establishment would like to see the creation of even more-effective ones. A spokesperson for the widely respected College of Physicians of Philadelphia sums it up, saying, "Researchers continue to explore new possibilities. Higher effectiveness, lower cost, and convenient delivery are some of the main goals."[35]

Pressure to Find New Vaccines

Both scientists and government officials in various nations remain constantly under pressure to achieve those goals, including making existing vaccines more available to those who need them the most. Meanwhile, the scientists who run the vaccine research labs are under pressure to find effective new vaccines for a wide range of illnesses that cause much misery and many deaths each year. One of the diseases for which new vaccines are constantly under development is influenza. Although some flu vaccines exist and are moderately effective, the viruses that cause the flu continue to mutate. As a result, researchers are constantly playing catch-up as they produce vaccines for each new flu strain that emerges.

Scientists would much prefer to find a universal flu vaccine that would not need to be changed each year. In fact, many immunologists feel it is urgent to find that universal vaccine. Sooner or later, some experts warn, a new flu mutation will appear and cause a pandemic (worldwide epidemic). Such a massive outbreak could kill millions of people in the course of only a few months.

Research also continues in the effort to develop vaccines for a host of other potentially deadly ailments. One is tuberculosis, a disease of the lungs that has plagued humanity for millennia and has a mortality rate of up to 50 percent. (That is, as many as half of those who contract it will die.) Human immunodeficiency virus,

A researcher in a Chinese lab checks a cell culture medium that will be used for studying vaccines for HIV. Governments throughout the world direct a massive amount of resources toward developing vaccines and curing diseases.

better known as HIV, is another disease for which researchers struggle to find a vaccine. The HIV virus can lead to AIDS, a condition that devastates a person's immune system, leaving him or her open to all sorts of damaging infections. Still other terrible maladies for which researchers try to develop vaccines are group A streptococcus, meningitis, Alzheimer's disease, cancer, and the Ebola and Zika viruses.

Ebola is a frightening disease because up to half of those who get it die from it. It first emerged in West Africa in 1976, and a later and larger outbreak occurred in 2013–2014 in which some twenty-nine thousand cases were reported. Immunologists naturally wanted to develop a vaccine to fight Ebola, but they first had to figure out how people became infected with it. WHO says, "Ebola is introduced into the human population through close contact with the blood, secretions, organs, or other bodily fluids of infected animals such as chimpanzees, gorillas, fruit bats, monkeys, forest antelope, and porcupines."[36]

Once a person contracts Ebola, medical authorities found, it typically ravages the body. It begins with fever and headaches and then progresses to vomiting, diarrhea, liver failure, and both internal and external bleeding. To keep people from suffering these dire symptoms, during the 2013–2014 outbreak medical authorities found and advised the public about ways to avoid catching it. First, they said, people should keep from touching the blood and body fluids (urine, saliva, sweat, and so forth) of someone who has the disease. Also, no one should handle items that may have been in contact with an infected person or his or her fluids. In addition, no one should directly touch the body of a person who has died from Ebola.

In 2016 a Canadian research lab managed to create a preliminary Ebola vaccine. Clinical trials conducted in 2017 and 2018 showed that the vaccine was only partially effective against the virus. So the researchers admitted that they had a long way to go before they could produce a completely effective vaccine.

Yet they were certain they were on the right track. In a novel approach, they started by studying a virus similar to Ebola that attacks cattle, horses, and pigs. They then replaced a key gene in that virus's DNA with a gene from the Ebola virus. The goal was to turn that tailored virus into a live attenuated vaccine that would fool the body into thinking it had been invaded by Ebola. In turn, the researchers hoped, an immune response would occur; yet someone injected with the vaccine would be safe because she or he cannot contract Ebola from a single gene. Work on refining that approach to a new vaccine continues.

Zika Spreads to the Americas

Like Ebola, Zika initially emerged to ravage humanity in modern times. First reported in 1947, Zika is primarily spread by

61

mosquitoes, which carry the virus in their saliva. For several decades following its discovery, the disease was confined to a small area of central Africa. Perhaps because it long remained local to that region, most research labs in the United States and other developed nations largely ignored it.

From 2007 to 2016, however, Zika suddenly spread across the Indian and Pacific Ocean regions to North and South America. One of the disease's principal dangers is its ability to pass from a pregnant mother to her unborn child. That fetus can suffer from severe brain damage and other birth defects. According to the Centers for Disease Control and Prevention:

> Congenital Zika syndrome is a unique pattern of birth defects found among fetuses and babies infected with Zika virus during pregnancy. Congenital Zika syndrome is described by the following five features: severe microcephaly [smaller than normal head] where the skull has partially collapsed; decreased brain tissue with a specific pattern of brain damage; damage (i.e., scarring, pigment changes) to the back of the eye; joints with limited range of motion, such as clubfoot; too much muscle tone restricting body movement soon after birth.
>
> [Also] babies who were infected with Zika before birth may have damage to their eyes and/or the part of their brain that is responsible for vision, which may affect their visual development.[37]

Early in the 2007–2016 outbreak of Zika, WHO called for the creation of a vaccine to protect against it. Eighteen labs situated in multiple countries immediately took on that task, and by 2017 both a killed vaccine and a subunit vaccine were under development. Scientists hope to produce a reliable vaccine against Zika by 2022 or 2023.

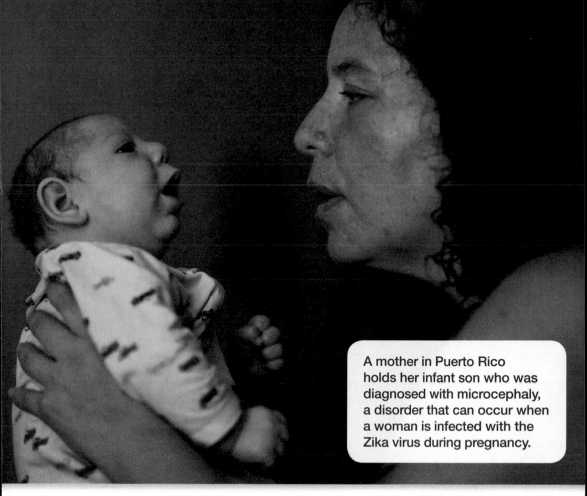

A mother in Puerto Rico holds her infant son who was diagnosed with microcephaly, a disorder that can occur when a woman is infected with the Zika virus during pregnancy.

The Goal of Preventing Cancer

While effective vaccines for Ebola and Zika may materialize in the near future, vaccines to prevent cancer are expected to take considerably longer. Research into cancer vaccines is well under way in various nations. But the challenges the researchers face are huge, for several reasons. First, the exact causes of cancer—in which normal bodily cells become abnormal and rapidly multiply and spread throughout the body—are still somewhat unclear. Second, humans are affected by more than one hundred different types of cancer, each of which has at least some distinct characteristics.

Third, and perhaps most important, immunologists are used to developing vaccines to protect against infectious diseases, but cancer is not an infectious disease caused by invading germs.

Preparing for Future Flu Pandemics

The dire effects of a lethal flu pandemic could in theory be considerably lessened by the development of an effective vaccine. Yet a new vaccine currently takes too long to create. If a pandemic strikes, that remedy will need to be available much more quickly. According to physician and CNN medical correspondent Sanjay Gupta:

> If we can develop and deploy a pandemic flu vaccine just 24 weeks faster than is currently projected, the impact could change the course of human history.
>
> Twenty-four weeks faster could mean the difference between 20,000 people dying in the next flu pandemic or more than 20 million people dying. . . .
>
> [WHO says that] in theory, we could make 5.4 billion doses of flu vaccine if we harnessed and aligned manufacturing facilities all over the world.
>
> Would it ever be possible, however, to create and distribute a vaccine 24 weeks faster—in six weeks instead of 30 weeks—and save more than 20 million lives?
>
> For starters, the way we typically make flu vaccine . . . hasn't changed much in nearly 70 years.
>
> We rely largely on hens' eggs to incubate and replicate the virus, which is too slow of a process to respond rapidly to pandemic flu. . . .
>
> It will take [much more] research and development money, as it always does, to bolster the techniques and infrastructure I described and make them available everywhere.
>
> And it will take accepting that a pandemic of flu is likely in our lifetime.

Sanjay Gupta, "The Big One Is Coming, and It's Going to Be a Flu Pandemic," CNN, April 7, 2014. www.cnn.com.

Instead, for reasons still only guessed at, the body can suddenly signal some of its normal cells to become abnormal and keep on multiplying. They can then form a cluster called a tumor, which in a majority of cases grows increasingly larger.

Despite being a noninfectious disease, however, cancer does display a few qualities that can aid immunologists in their quest for a vaccine. For example, cancer cells do display antigens, in the form of individual proteins, on their outer surfaces. One problem that researchers have encountered is that in most kinds of cancer, those antigens are invisible, or nearly so, to the antibodies the immune system sends to fight substances that pose a threat to the body. This explains why a cancerous tumor can grow bigger and bigger and not trigger a defense by the immune system.

Some progress has been made in recent decades toward inducing the antigens on cancer cells to become visible to the immune system. But a resulting "antigen vaccine" still remains years away from becoming a realistic protection against cancer. Meanwhile, some researchers are working on a different approach. They are attempting to make a vaccine that would signal the immune system's antibodies to attack the stroma, the connective tissue located between any two cancer cells. One thing that makes this idea promising is that the stroma makes up roughly 60 percent of a typical cancerous tumor. Also, without the stroma, a tumor cannot grow beyond microscopic size; and a microscopic tumor that cannot grow larger is harmless to the body.

Still another model for a cancer vaccine that some research labs are using revolves around developing DNA vaccines to fight cancer. In this approach, the scientists begin with a virus and by various means render it harmless. The next step is to alter the virus's DNA in such a way that it recognizes a specific antigen on the surface of a particular kind of cancer. Those steps are already doable. The hard part, which is not yet perfected, is to inject the virus into a patient and stimulate his or her normal cells to manufacture antigens that look like those of the cancer. In theory, this would hopefully motivate the immune system to produce large numbers of T cells to attack the cancer.

These and the several other approaches immunologists are employing to produce cancer vaccines are made difficult by a number of factors. By far the most frustrating factor is the simple

> "[Researchers are] trying to identify the mechanisms by which cancer cells evade or suppress anticancer immune responses."[38]
>
> —National Cancer Institute

reality that for reasons still unclear, cancer cells are able to steer clear of potential attacks by the immune system. Until scientists can fully understand why this occurs, they will not be able to make an effective cancer vaccine. The National Cancer Institute says that researchers are "trying to identify the mechanisms by which cancer cells evade or suppress anticancer immune responses. A better understanding of how cancer cells manipulate the immune system could lead to the development of drugs that block those processes, thereby improving the effectiveness of cancer treatment vaccines."[38]

Vaccines in a Banana?

In addition to working on new vaccines to fight specific diseases, immunologists and other scientists are also working on new ways to administer those helpful substances. Already, a nasal spray can be used to deliver flu vaccine to children. Another novel approach to delivering vaccines is to make them edible. One of the chief proponents of this idea is Arizona State University scientist Charles Arntzen. When Arntzen visited Thailand in 1993, one expert observer writes,

> he was not expecting a moment of scientific "eureka" that would redirect his career. However, after observing a young Thai mother soothing her fussy infant with bits of banana, this plant molecular biologist was struck with an idea that is both startling and ingenious. What if, in addition to quieting her child, the mother could also administer a life-saving vaccine *in the banana*?[39]

The basic idea behind an edible vaccine is to combine DNA from the target disease microbe with the genetic materials of an edible plant. A person eats the plant containing the altered DNA (either in a meal or in pill form), and his or her immune system detects the illness's genetic materials. Ideally, an appropriate immune response follows, and the person gains immunity to the disease.

There are several potential benefits to using edible vaccines. First, most disease germs enter the body through the moist mucous membranes that surround the intestines and other internal organs and extend to the eyes and insides of the nose and mouth. When someone eats a vaccine-laden plant food, the digestive system breaks it down and releases the disease-altered disease gene to the mucous membranes. This triggers a more immediate and stronger immune response, like the kind generated by an injected vaccine.

Another benefit of edible vaccines is that the plants used can be grown locally, and local labs can make the vaccines. This saves on the costs of shipping both the plants and vaccines from other regions. Also, and importantly, no needles would be involved.

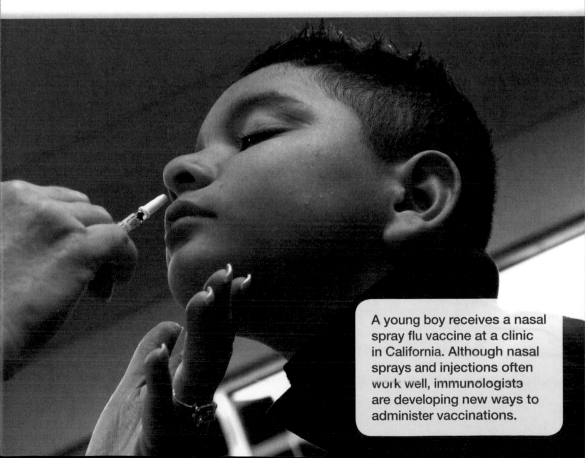

A young boy receives a nasal spray flu vaccine at a clinic in California. Although nasal sprays and injections often work well, immunologists are developing new ways to administer vaccinations.

Chris Spinelli lightheartedly but accurately points out, "Too many people just don't like needles!"[40]

Although virtually all immunologists acknowledge the potential advantages of edible vaccines, they also realize that a number of obstacles to making them a reality still exist. First, preliminary research shows that disease genes that are combined with plant genes produce too weak an immune response. So a way must be found to increase the potency of the altered DNA. Also, at present, the process of altering the plants' genetic materials is too time-consuming and expensive. In addition, some Americans and Europeans fear that so-called genetically modified foods might pose their own risks. That worry has significantly reduced the

Genome Editing Is Fast Approaching

The potential of using gene editing to do the same thing vaccines do is real. As an article in the February 2018 issue of the *Lancet* medical journal says, "The international race to bring human genome editing into widespread use in clinical medicine is moving fast." Indeed, on January 23, 2018, the National Institutes of Health Common Fund launched its so-called Somatic Cell Genome Editing program. Its estimated initial cost was $190 million, to be spent over the course of six years to develop genome editing into realistic medical practice.

Despite this ongoing project, the *Lancet* article points out, China was already ahead of the United States in the area of genome editing. Perhaps as many as eighty-six people in China had already had their genes altered by 2018, the article said. In comparison, the US Food and Drug Administration only began enrolling test patients for its program in the same year. There were a number of concerns among American scientists that, as they moved forward with the new technology, they would encounter questions about safety issues. Nevertheless, the US program did continue to move forward, as did the Chinese efforts and similar research in Europe. Thus, the *Lancet* emphasizes, "Human genome editing is no longer a concept confined to the pages of futuristic science fiction novels—modifying genetic code is here now and is advancing rapidly."

Lancet, "Editing the Human Genome: Balancing Safety and Regulation," February 3, 2018, p. 402.

amount of funding available for vigorous research and development of edible vaccines.

Toward a World Without Vaccines

Interestingly, it is conceivable that by the time scientists overcome these difficulties and can produce plenty of effective edible vaccines, traditional vaccines themselves may have become obsolete. This startling concept is based on the reality that genome editing is a rapidly developing technology. Genome editing is the process of manipulating the DNA in the genes of humans or animals. In theory, it alters the genetic code, producing a host of possible physical and other changes.

Several scientists who are working on the technology predict that once perfected, this approach could, among other things, do the same thing that vaccines do—namely, protect people from harmful diseases. That is, genome editing could make a person immune to various ailments without the need for vaccination. This could be done, those experts say,

"Genetic manipulation could negate the need for vaccines as we know them!"[42]

—Doctor and medical researcher Chris Spinelli

by cutting out a segment of a person's DNA and replacing it with a fragment of DNA that makes him or her resistant or immune to a given disease. As Craig Mello, winner of the Nobel Prize in Physiology or Medicine, explains, science could find "a way of improving and repairing and making genes better, safer, and healthier." Eventually, he goes on, "it may be like vaccination, where, if you have a child, you'll want to have these [genetic] tests done and perhaps have a correction made."[41]

If genome editing is ever perfected, as well as accepted by the general public, Spinelli writes, there will be "a change in human beings that will affect how we view and use vaccines." Whether it happens in a century or more, or a mere few decades from now, Spinelli says, "genetic manipulation could negate the need for vaccines as we know them!"[42]

SOURCE NOTES

Introduction: The Miracle at Melun

1. Kristen A. Feemster, *Vaccines: What Everyone Needs to Know*. New York: Oxford University Press, 2018, p. 1.
2. Quoted in René Valery-Radot, *The Life of Pasteur*, trans. R.L Devonshire. Charleston, SC: Bibliolife, 2008, p. 120.
3. Quoted in Valery-Radot, *The Life of Pasteur*, p. 124.
4. Quoted in Madeleine P. Grant, *Louis Pasteur: Fighting Hero of Science*. New York: McGraw-Hill, 1960, p. 67.
5. Quoted in Grant, *Louis Pasteur*, p. 67.
6. National Health Service, "How Vaccines Save Lives," April 4, 2016. www.nhs.uk.

Chapter 1: Flickers of Hope in a Disease-Ravaged World

7. Jennifer Wright, *Get Well Soon: History's Worst Plagues and the Heroes Who Fought Them*. New York: Henry Holt, 2017, pp. 10–11.
8. *Medical Daily*, "A Brief History of Vaccines: From Medieval Chinese 'Variolation' to Modern Vaccination," 2018. www.medicaldaily.com.
9. Quoted in *Modern History Sourcebook*, "Lady Mary Wortley Montagu: Smallpox Vaccination in Turkey," 1998. www.fordham.edu.
10. Quoted in *Modern History Sourcebook*, "Lady Mary Wortley Montagu."
11. Edward Jenner, "An Inquiry into the Causes and Effects of the Variole Vaccine, or Cow-Pox, 1798," Lit2Go. http://etc.usf.edu.
12. Jenner, "An Inquiry into the Causes and Effects of the Variole Vaccine, or Cow-Pox, 1798."

13. Jenner, "An Inquiry into the Causes and Effects of the Variole Vaccine, or Cow-Pox, 1798."

Chapter 2: Discovering How the Immune System Works

14. Ananya Mandal, "What Is a Macrophage?," News-Medical .net, January 14, 2014. www.news-medical.net.
15. Jennifer Acckerman, "How Not to Fight Colds," *New York Times*, October 5, 2010. www.nytimes.com.
16. Wright, *Get Well Soon*, p. 249.
17. World Health Organization, "Diphtheria," 2018. www.who.int.
18. Quoted in Harold Faber and Doris Faber, *American Heroes of the 20th Century*. New York: Random House, 1967, p. 71.
19. FDR 4 Freedoms Project, "Polio & Paralysis: Franklin D. Roosevelt's Disability." http://fdr4freedoms.org.
20. Meredith Wadman, *The Vaccine Race: Science, Politics, and the Human Costs of Defeating Disease*. New York: Viking, 2017, pp. 7–8.

Chapter 3: Triumph over a Host of Deadly Maladies

21. Feemster, *Vaccines*, p. 31.
22. National Institutes of Health, "Vaccine Types," April 3, 2012. www.niaid.nih.gov.
23. US Department of Health and Human Services, "HPV (Human Papillomavirus)," 2018. www.vaccines.gov.
24. Quoted in Issie Lapowsky, "The Next Big Thing You Missed: This Mosquito-Dissecting, Malaria-Killing Robot Needs Your Help," *Wired*, June 3, 2014. www.wired.com.
25. US Department of Health and Human Services, "Measles," 2018. www.vaccines.gov.
26. F.E. Andre et al., "Vaccination Greatly Reduces Disease, Disability, Death and Inequity Worldwide," World Health Organization, 2018. www.who.int.

Chapter 4: A Modern Backlash Against Vaccination

27. Quoted in Kelley King Heyworth, "Vaccines: The Reality Behind the Debate," *Parents*, 2018. www.parents.com.
28. Heyworth, "Vaccines."
29. Feemster, *Vaccines*, p. xx.

30. Quoted in Heyworth, "Vaccines."
31. Feemster, *Vaccines*, p. 13.
32. Feemster, *Vaccines*, p. 90.
33. Centers for Disease Control and Prevention, "Parents' Guide to Childhood Immunizations, Part 4," September 20, 2016. www.cdc.gov.
34. Chris Spinelli and Maryann Karinch, *The Vaccine Debate: Making the Right Choice for You and Your Children*. Far Hills, NJ: New Horizon, 2015, p. 194.

Chapter 5: New Research and the Future of Vaccines

35. College of Physicians of Philadelphia, "The Future of Immunization," January 10, 2018. www.historyofvaccines.org.
36. World Health Organization, "Ebola Virus Disease," 2018. www.who.int.
37. Centers for Disease Control and Prevention, "Microcephaly and Other Birth Defects," March 1, 2018. www.cdc.gov.
38. National Cancer Institute, "Cancer Vaccines," December 8, 2015. www.cancer.gov.
39. Quoted in Redig Mandy, "Banana Vaccines: A Conversation with Dr. Charles Arntzen," *Journal of Young Investigators*, September 6, 2005. www.jyi.org.
40. Spinelli and Karinch, *The Vaccine Debate*, p. 188.
41. Craig Mello, "Re-engineering Human Embryos," *On Point*, National Public Radio, April 28, 2015. www.wbur.org.
42. Spinelli and Karinch, *The Vaccine Debate*, p. 169.

GLOSSARY

antibodies: Proteins manufactured by the body's white blood cells to defend against invading disease germs.

antigen: A harmful substance, most often a disease microbe that invades the body.

attenuation: The weakening of harmful disease germs for use in a vaccine.

culture: A laboratory growth of germs for medical study.

DNA vaccine: A vaccine that uses pieces of genetic material called DNA from harmful germs to stimulate human cells to create an immune response.

immune response: The body's defensive reaction to harmful substances that invade it from the outside.

inoculation: The practice of injecting the body with a form of a disease to ward off future attacks of that disease.

killed vaccine: A vaccine made of microbes that have been rendered harmless by killing them.

live vaccine: A vaccine made of living germs.

lymphocyte: A white blood cell that creates or aids in the making of the body's defensive forces during an immune response.

strain: A variation of a specific kind of disease germ.

subunit vaccine: A vaccine made of disease antigens that have been artificially altered by being grown in cultures of harmless germs.

synthetic peptide vaccine: A vaccine made of artificial chemical copies of parts of microscopic parasites.

toxoid vaccine: A vaccine made of antitoxins.

vaccine: A substance that provides protection against a specific disease by triggering the body's natural immune system without passing on the disease itself.

Books

Tara Haelle, *Vaccination Investigation: The History and Science of Vaccines*. Minneapolis: Twenty-First Century, 2018.

Vic Kovacs, *Vaccines*. New York: Gareth Stevens, 2017.

Noel Merino, *Vaccines*. Farmington Hills, MI: Greenhaven, 2015.

Rhythm Prism, *Jonas Salk*. Charleston, SC: Amazon Digital Services, 2014.

Pete Schauer, *AIDS and Other Killer Viruses and Pandemics*. New York: Greenhaven, 2018.

Internet Sources

Centers for Disease Control and Prevention, "Pregnancy and Vaccination," August 5, 2016. www.cdc.gov/vaccines/pregnancy/pregnant-women/index.html.

Matthew F. Daley and Jason M. Glanz, "Straight Talk About Vaccination," *Scientific American*, August 24, 2011. www.scientificamerican.com/article/straight-talk-about-vaccination.

Cynthia Gorney, "Here's Why Vaccines Are So Crucial," *National Geographic*, November 2017. www.nationalgeographic.com/magazine/2017/11/vaccine-health-infection-global-children.

Will Greenberg, "More Parents Are Refusing to Vaccinate Their Kids—but Not for the Reason You Think," *Mother Jones*, August 29, 2016. www.motherjones.com/environment/2016/08/there-are-more-anti-vax-parents-doctors-offices.

Luke Mullins, "Dr. Hoffman vs. the Mosquito," *Washingtonian*, October 23, 2013. www.washingtonian.com/2013/10/23/dr-hoffman-vs-the-mosquito.

National Cancer Institute, "Cancer Vaccines," December 18, 2015. www.cancer.gov/about-cancer/causes-prevention/vaccines-fact-sheet.

US Food and Drug Administration, "Flu Vaccines," March 3, 2015. www.fda.gov/BiologicsBloodVaccines/Vaccines/QuestionsaboutVaccines/ucm070414.htm.

US Health and Human Services, "Measles," 2018. www.vaccines.gov/diseases/measles/index.html.

WebMD, "Whooping Cough Vaccine: FAQ," April 22, 2016. www.webmd.com/children/vaccines/whooping-cough-and-the-dtap-vaccine.

Websites

History of Vaccines (www.historyofvaccines.org). Philadelphia's famed College of Physicians has put together an enormously informative, accurate, and useful site about vaccines, including a timeline and links to numerous relevant articles and fact boxes.

Vaccines—Calling the Shots, *Nova* (www.pbs.org/wgbh/nova/body/vaccines-calling-shots.html). The award-wining *Nova* team created this excellent website, which features links to many articles related to the present state of vaccination in the United States, including recent increases in vaccine hesitancy among some parents.

Vaccines, World Health Organization (www.who.int/topics/vaccines/en). This informative site provides numerous links to facts on current vaccine research and development, vaccine safety issues, information about vaccines for children and infants, and much more.

Note: Boldface page numbers indicate illustrations.

Ackerman, Jannifer, 25
allergic reactions, severe, 55
anaphylaxis, 55
anthrax, vaccine for, 7–9, **9**, 20
antibodies, **24**
  B and T cells and, 23
  cancer antigens and, 65
  function of, 23–24
  messenger chemicals and, 35–36
  produced by vaccines, 7
antigens
  antibodies and, 23–24
  B cells and, 24–25
  cancer and, 65
  toxins, 28–29
antitoxins, 28–29, **29**
anti-vaxxers, 46–47, **47**, 48–50, 55–56, 57
Arntzen, Charles, 66
attenuation, principle of, 7
autism, 46–47, 49–52

bacteria, 19
B cells, 23, 24–25

cancer, 63–66
Caroline (princess of England), 14–15
Centers for Disease Control and Prevention (CDC), 56, 62
Cervarix, 41
chicken cholera, 7
chicken pox, 45
China, inoculation in ancient, 13

cold viruses, 25
cowpox, 16–18, **17**
Crick, Francis, 35

deoxyribonucleic acid (DNA)
  genome editing, 69
  heredity and, 35
  vaccines, 35–37, 65
diphtheria, 28–29, **29**
diseases
  germs as principal agents of, 6, 10, 19–20
  immunity to, explained, 24–25
  miasmas as cause of, 10
  mutation in form of, 15
  as punishment for sins, 11
  unsanitary practices and, 11–12, **12**

Ebola, 60–61
eczema, 55
edible vaccines, 66–69
Ehrlich, Paul, 23
electron microscopes, importance of, 26
"engrafting," 14
Estall, Lisa, 50
Estall, Summer, 50

fainting, 56
febrile seizures, 55
Feemster, Kristen A.
  on action of vaccines, 7
  on changes in vaccine development, 34
  on importance of education about vaccination, 48

on *Lancet* retraction of Wakefield's
paper, 52
on Wakefield, 52
fermentation, 19
flu, 37–38, 59, 64
Francis, Thomas, 33

Gardasil, 41
genome editing, 68, 69
germs
DNA of, 35–36
inactivated ("killed"), as basis of
vaccines, 27, 30, 38
live attenuated, as basis of
vaccines, 20–21, 25–26
mutation of, 15
as principal agents of diseases, 6,
10, 19–20
toxins produced by, 28
germ theory, 6, 10
GlaxoSmithKline, 41
Grancher, Jacques, 21
Gupta, Sanjay, 64

hepatitis B, **36**, 37
herd immunity, 47–48
Hoffman, Stephen, 42, 43
"How I Became Anti-vaccine" (blog),
49
human genome editing, 68, 69
human immunodeficiency virus (HIV),
59–60, **60**
human papilloma virus (HPV), 39–41,
40
hydrophobia, 20–21, **21**

immune response, 23, **24**, 25–26
immune system
genome editing and, 69
natural versus artificial immunity,
24–25
using, in cancer vaccine, 65–66
vaccines and, 7, 23–24
immunology, defined, 22
infantile paralysis, 22, 29–33, **32**
influenza, 37–38, 59, 64

inoculation. *See* vaccines

Jenner, Edward
cowpox inoculations, 16–18, **17**
importance of, 21
viral mutations ideas of, 15

Lancet (medical journal), 48–50, 68
lymphocytes, 23

macrophages, 23–24
malaria, 42–43, **43**
Mandal, Ananya, 23–24
March of Dimes, 31
McCarthy, Jenny, 47
measles, 44–45, 53–54
Medical Daily (online medical
newsletter), 13
Meister, Joseph, 21
Mello, Craig, 69
Merck Sharpe and Dohme, 37, 41
messenger chemicals, 35–36
Metchnikoff, Élie, 23
miasmas, 10
microbes. *See* germs
microscopes, 26
MMR vaccine, 44–45, 51
MMRV vaccine, 45
Montagu, Lady Mary Wortley, 13–14
mumps, 45
mutations, 15

nasal sprays, 66, **67**
National Cancer Institute, 40–41, 66
National Foundation for Infantile
Paralysis, 31–32
National Health Service (Britain), 9
National Institutes of Health, 37
National Institutes of Health Common
Fund, 68
National Vaccine Injury
Compensation Program, 53, 57
New York Times (newspaper), 25

Olshansky, S. Jay, 45
Oprah Winfrey Show, The, 47

optical microscopes, 26

Parents (magazine), 50
Pasteur, Louis
  germs as principal agents of
    diseases, 6
  importance of, 21
  inactivated germs and, 27
  vaccines for
    anthrax and, 7–9, **9**, 20
    chicken cholera and, 7
    rabies, 20–21, **21**
  wine spoilage studies, 6, 19–20
pertussis, 38–39
Phipps, James, **17**, 17–18
Pike, Eileen, 47
polio, 22, 29–33, **32**
Population Reference Bureau, 39
protozoan infections, 42–43

rabies, 20–21, **21**
research
  challenges to, 58–59
  on methods of administration of
    vaccines, 66–69
  for universal flu vaccine, 59
  on vaccines for
    cancer, 63–66
    Ebola, 60–61
    HIV, 59–60, **60**
    tuberculosis, 59
    Zika, 61–62, **63**
Romania, 54
Roosevelt, Franklin D., 31
Rossignol, Hippolyte, 8, 9
rubella, 45
Ruska, Ernst, 26

Sabin, Albert B., 30
Salk, Jonas, 30, **32**, 32–33
seizures, 55
sexually transmitted diseases,
  39–41, **40**
smallpox
  cowpox and immunity to, 16–18,
    17

inoculation against, 13–15
Somatic Cell Genome Editing
  program, 68
Spinelli, Chris
  on administration of vaccines, 68
  on arguments for and against
    vaccination, 57
  on genome editing, 69
Stevens-Johnson syndrome, 55
stroma, 65
subunit vaccines
  described, 35–37
  for HPV, 41
  for pertussis (whooping cough),
    38–39
synthetic peptides, 41–43, **43**

T cells and antibodies, 23
toxins, 28–29
toxoid vaccines, 28–29
tuberculosis, 59

unsanitary practices and diseases,
  11–12, **12**
US Department of Health and
  Human Services
  on HPV infections, 39–40
  on measles, 44
  National Vaccine Injury
    Compensation Program claims
    and, 57
US Department of Justice, 57
US Food and Drug Administration,
  68

vaccination
  backlash by parents against
    decline in rates of, and, 46,
      52–53
    effects of, 47–48, 53–54, **54**
    medical establishment reaction
      to, 50–52, **51**
    reasons given for, 46–47, **47**,
      48–50, 55–56, 57
  early practices, 13–15
  importance of education about, 48

reasons for, 44, 57
    decline in childhood mortality,
        33, 44
    eradication of diseases, 9, 45
    herd immunity for society,
        47–48
    social and economic benefits, 44
side effects, 55–56
vaccines
    development of
        anthrax, 7–9, **9**, 20
        chicken cholera, 7
        cost of, 58–59
        diphtheria, 28–29, **29**
        focus on safety, 34–37
        hepatitis B, **36**, 37
        HPV, **40**, 40–41
        influenza, 37–38
        live attenuated germs as basis,
            45
        malaria, 42–43, **43**
        measles, mumps, and rubella,
            44–45, 51
        pertussis (whooping cough),
            38–39
        rabies, 20–21, **21**
        smallpox, 13–18, **17**
        varicella (chicken pox), 45
    DNA, 35, 65
    inactivated ("killed") germs as
        basis, 27, 30, 38

live attenuated germs as basis,
    20–21, 25–26
for local diseases, 58
motivation of immune system by,
    7, 23–24
subunit, 35, 38–39, 41
synthetic peptides, 41–43, **43**
term coined, 18
toxoid, 28–29
vaccinia virus, 55
varicella (chicken pox), 45

Wadman, Meredith, 33
Wakefield, Andrew, 48–50, 52
Watson, James, 35
whooping cough, 38–39
wine spoilage, 6, 19–20
Woodford, Chris, 26
World Health Organization (WHO)
    on diphtheria, 28
    on Ebola, 60–61
    on importance of vaccines, 45
    on malaria, 42
    on social and economic benefits of
        vaccines, 44
    on time needed to make flu
        vaccine, 64
    Zika and, 62
Wright, Jennifer, 11, 27

Zika, 61–62, **63**

PICTURE CREDITS

Cover: Creativa Images/Shutterstock.com

4: rook76/Shutterstock.com (bottom left)

4: Everett Historical/Shutterstock.com (bottom right)

4: Everett Historical/Shutterstock.com (top)

5: PictureLake/iStockphoto.com (top left)

5: fotohunter/Shutterstock.com (top right)

5: Image Point Fr/Shutterstock.com (bottom)

9: Album/Prisma/Newscom

12: The Black Death (gouache on paper), Nicolle, Pat (Patrick) (1907–95)/ Private Collection/© Look and Learn/Bridgeman Images

17: Edward Jenner (1749–1823) performing the first vaccination against Smallpox in 1796, 1879 (oil on canvas) (detail) (see also 166614), Melingue, Gaston (1840–1914)/Academie Nationale de Medecine, Paris, France/Archives Charmet/Bridgeman Images

21: Louis Pasteur experimenting for the cure of hydrophobia in his laboratory, c.1885, pub. c.1895 (print), Marie, Adrien Emmanuel (1848–91) (after)/Private Collection/Bridgeman Images

24: David Mack/Science Source

29: Making diphtheria serum from horse blood, from "Les Animaux," c.1900 (colour litho), French School (20th century)/Musee d'Histoire de la Medecine, Paris, France/Archives Charmet/Bridgeman Images

32: Dr. Jonas Salk Giving Vaccine (b/w photo)/Underwood Archives/UIG/ Bridgeman Images

36: Volker Steger/Science Source

40: sirtravelalot/Shutterstock.com

43: Burger/Phanie/Science Source

47: Associated Press

51: Associated Press

54: Del Puppo/Fotogramma/Ropi/ZUMA Press/Newscom

60: CHINE NOUVELLE/SIPA/Newscom

63: Associated Press

67: Ana Venegas/ZUMA Press/Newscom